D1496756

Limits of Loyalty

Edited by
Edgar Denton III

Wilfrid Laurier University Press

Canadian Cataloguing in Publication Data

Military History Symposium (Canada), 6th, Royal
Military College, 1979.
  Limits of loyalty

Proceedings of the sixth Military History Symposium,
held at the Royal Military College, Kingston,
Ont., 1979.

Includes index.

ISBN 0-88920-091-2 bd.

1. Military ethics – Congresses. 2. Allegiance –
Congresses. I. Denton, Edgar, 1919-   II. Title

U22.M54   355.1'23   C80-094262-0

Copyright © 1980
WILFRID LAURIER UNIVERSITY PRESS
Waterloo, Ontario, Canada   N2L 3C5
80 81 82 83 4 3 2 1

Cover Design: David Antscherl

CONTENTS

PREFACE

THE SIXTH Royal Military College History Symposium continued the pattern of a broad interpretation of the subject which was set in 1974 when the topic was Military Reconstruction in Post-War Societies. Succeeding sessions were devoted to Soldiers as Statesmen in the Twentieth Century (1975), War Aims and Strategy: The Great War, 1914-1918 (1976), General Staffs and Diplomacy: The Decade Before the Second World War (1977), and Regular Armies and Insurgency (1978).

Limits of Loyalty, the topic of the 1979 Symposium continued in the direction charted in 1978. From that discussion it was apparent that one of the major problems in a potentially explosive situation is the attitude of a state's armed forces toward the existing regime. Hence, where the 1978 discussion had focussed on the military actions of Regular Forces, the 1979 symposium discussed the dilemma facing military and naval officers, not only when there are great differences between a "higher law" and the apparent requirements of the nation-state, but also where there is a conflict between the governing regime—the state, and at least a large segment of the population—the nation, and there is a possibility that the "Insurgents" are "right." The topics were chosen to provide a broad chronological view of a variety of instances of this dilemma beginning with the American Revolution. Although the keynote address set a frame for the succeeding papers, there was no attempt to extract "laws" from the five cases. Emphasis was rather on each case as a unique situation. Individually and collectively they generated much productive discussion, and are presented here in the hope that they will serve as a basis for further consideration.

The Symposium could not have been held without the direct financial support of the Department of National Defence. Nor could it have succeeded without the whole-hearted cooperation of the National Defence College and Canadian Forces Base Kingston in providing many essential support services. Particular thanks must be given to R.M.C.'s Commandant, Brigadier-General A. J. G. D. de Chastelain,

for his interest and encouragement. His officers and Staff cooperated
with cheerful help to meet every administrative and organization problem. Lieutenant-Colonel Frank Hlohovsky, Director of Administration; Captain Gord Johnson, Administrative Officer; Mr. Fawkes and
Sergeant Breland of the Senior Staff Mess; Sergeant McFarlane and
Mrs. Norleen Hope of the Transport Section were particularly helpful.
The many details which plague any conference were effortlessly handled by Dr. R. G. Haycock, Captain Serge Bernier, and in particular
Mrs. Karen Brown of the History Department.

This publication is the result of expeditious and thorough attention
to all the editorial and administrative details by Dr. Harold Remus,
Director of Wilfrid Laurier University Press, and Janet Kaethler and
Marlene Hickson who cheerfully guided the Symposium Director
through the intricacies of preparing the manuscript.

Most important of all, we must express our appreciation to the
speakers for stimulating presentations, and to the other participants
for their penetrating questions and comments.

EDGAR DENTON III
Symposium Director

CONTRIBUTORS

George F. G. Stanley is Emeritus Professor of Canadian Studies at Mount Allison University. He was educated at the University of Alberta and at Oxford University, where he was a Rhodes Scholar, and from which he received the D.Phil. in 1935. After service as a Lieutenant-Colonel during World War II he was Professor of History and Dean of Arts at The Royal Military College of Canada from 1949 to 1969. He has received Guggenheim and Canada Council Fellowships and in 1955-1956 was President of the Canadian Historical Association. He is an Officer of the Order of Canada. His writings include *Canada's Soldiers; New France, the Last Phase* and *Canada Invaded, 1775-1776*.

Ira D. Gruber is Professor of History at Rice University and a student of the War for American Independence. He was born in Philadelphia and educated at Duke University. He has been a Fellow at the Institute of Early American History and Culture and has taught at William and Mary, Occidental College, and, since 1966, at Rice University. Currently on leave from Rice, he is serving as John F. Morrison Professor of Military History at the U.S. Army Command and General Staff College, Fort Leavenworth. His publications include *The Howe Brothers and the American Revolution* (New York, 1972) as well as a series of articles on the origins of British strategy in the American War.

Samuel F. Scott received his Ph.D. from the University of Wisconsin in 1968 and is presently an Associate Professor of History at Wayne State University in Detroit. He has done research in France under the auspices of grants from the Social Science Research Council and National Endowment for the Humanities. Articles of his have appeared in *Annales historiques de la Révolution française* (1968 and 1972), *The Journal of Modern History* (1970), and *The American Historical Review* (1975); among his most recent publications is *The Response of the Royal Army to the French Revolution* (Oxford, 1978). His current research includes French aid to the American Revolution and the transformation of the French Army in the late eighteenth century.

Gunther E. Rothenberg is Professor of Military History at Purdue University. He served with the British Army during World War II, and with the U.S. Air Force until 1955. He received his Ph.D. from the University of Illinois and was a Guggenheim Fellow in 1962-63. His publications include *The Army of Francis-Joseph* (W. Lafayette, 1976), and *The Anatomy of the Israeli Army* (London and New York, 1979). He currently is co-researcher and editor of the Project on War and Society in East Central Europe.

Desmond Morton is Professor of History at the University of Toronto and the former Vice-Principal (Academic) at Erindale College. A graduate of The Royal Military College in 1959, he is the author of several books on Canadian military and political history including *Ministers and Generals: Politics and the Canadian Militia, The Last War Drum,* and *The Canadian General: Sir William Otter.*

Peter Hoffmann holds the Chair for German History at McGill University. Educated in Germany, he received the Dr. phil. (Modern History) from the University of Munich in 1961. He has received numerous Canada Council grants since 1971. His writings include *The History of the German Resistance 1933-1945* (London and Cambridge, 1977), *Hitler's Personal Security* (London and Cambridge, 1979), and *Widerstand gegen Hitler* (Munich, 1979). He is currently working on a study dealing with Stauffenberg.

OBEDIENCE TO WHOM? TO WHAT?

G. F. G. STANLEY

1

IN ONE of the essays in his book *On Moral Courage*, the Scottish novelist, Compton Mackenzie, tells the story of William Douglas Home, a younger brother of Lord Home, British Secretary of State for Foreign Affairs in August 1944. Educated at Eton and Oxford, William Home was a strong supporter of Prime Minister Neville Chamberlain, whose action in going to see Adolph Hitler at Munich in an effort to preserve peace in Europe, he greatly admired. Called up for military service in 1940, William Home was sent to Officer Cadet Training Unit (OCTU) for officer training, being posted, as one might expect, to the Brigade of Guards squad at Sandhurst. After receiving his commission, Home was posted to an armoured regiment, where he trained on Churchill tanks. On several occasions he was given leave to contest by-elections. He did reasonably well but did not, however, succeed in winning a seat in the British House of Commons.

In 1943 William Home was very much disturbed by the Churchill-Roosevelt decision at Casablanca not to negotiate with Germany and to accept nothing less than unconditional surrender. In Home's opinion such unyielding terms would not only prolong the war, but would put an end to any hope of securing "a stable political future" for the world.[1] That unconditional surrender was a "disastrous blunder" was confirmed, in Home's opinion, by the failure of the Allies to give their open support to the plot on the part of certain German officers to assassinate Hitler.[2] Home proposed to resign his commission by way of protest. When his request for his release was refused, he wrote a letter to the press expressing his strong criticism of his government's policy. Beyond receiving a scolding from his commanding officer, no further steps were taken to discipline Home for what was unquestionably a breach of good soldierly behaviour.

Finally, just before the British assault upon Le Havre, Home found himself faced with what he looked upon as a major moral issue. The German commander at Le Havre had approached the British, asking permission to evacuate a large number of French civilians from

[1] Compton Mackenzie, *On Moral Courage* (London, 1962), p. 141.
[2] Ibid., p. 142.

the city. There was, apparently, ample time to do so, since the British attack was not scheduled to go in for several days. But permission was refused, and Home was, along with the other officers of his regiment, ordered to take part in the operation. These are Home's own words:

> Faced with what I considered to be an immoral order, I must either obey it and abandon what I had conceived to be the humanitarian fight that I had waged so long—thus proving myself afraid to prac- tise what I preached, or I must disobey it and face the unknown fate that would be mine.[3]

After spending the night arguing with himself, he refused to take part in the assault, which incidentally saw some 12,000 civilians killed—unnecessarily killed, Home believed—as a result of air bom- bardment. He therefore sat down and wrote another letter to the press. Ironically, on the day his letter appeared in print, the German com- mander at Calais requested and received permission to evacuate French civilians from the battle area. Nevertheless, Home's second letter to the press left the military authorities no choice but to bring him before a court-martial. He was found guilty of disobeying a military order—not that of refusing to take part in the assault upon Le Havre, but of writing to the press without permission. He was cashiered and sentenced to twelve months' hard labour in Wormwood Scrubs prison. The punishment might have been worse.

Home knew that he would be punished. He knew, too, that his breach of discipline would excite strong disapproval on the part of the British public, if only because he belonged to a class of society which, traditionally, was expected to embody the principles of authority and discipline, especially in time of war. To express what others were bound to regard as unpatriotic criticism was, therefore, a particularly difficult decision for Home to make. Perhaps, had the War Office ignored his letter, he might have appeared, if not to his contemporaries then at least to a later generation, as little more than a vain, self- opinionated young man; instead of which he took on the heroic pro- portions of a man, not only of conviction, but of great moral courage. Here is what William Home wrote about this episode:

> Time and again, I have been called a fool for writing it. Time and again, I have heard people say that if I had not written it, I would not have been sent to prison or cashiered. Time and again, I have been told that my military superiors had very likely decided that, even if my action was not justified (and perhaps they even thought it was), it was at least to be expected of me in a situation of that kind. And, time and again, I have tried to explain that my personal position was not my chief concern. I was, at that time, on fire with crusading zeal. I wanted, above everything, to advertise my action, not from an exhibi-

---

[3] Ibid., p. 144.

tionist motive (as my enemies no doubt alleged), but because the voice within me shouted to be heard. . . . I hoped that an exposure of the situation at Le Havre would help to make the public see that all our propaganda was one-sided and dishonest and inevitably calculated to prolong the war. . . .[4]

Compton Mackenzie was not the only imaginative writer who ever explored the issue of what he regarded as one of moral courage against moral cowardice. Sophocles did the same thing in his fourth-century-B.C. play *Antigone,* in which he dealt with the conflict between a woman's conscience and the law of the state; twenty-four centuries later, Hermann Wouk did the same thing in his novel *The Caine Mutiny,* which dealt with an American naval officer's refusal to obey the orders of an incompetent superior.

But there are other eyes than those of the novelist or playwright through which to look at the issue of obedience and disobedience; the question may be viewed from the standpoint of the jurist, the philosopher, and the political scientist. And the issue itself. Is it simply a matter of moral courage, or is it one of law, morals, or politics?

2

IN 1960 a young American air force pilot, Francis Gary Powers, was brought before a Russian military tribunal on a charge of aerial espionage. Asked whether he had ever considered the possibility that his U-2 flight might provoke hostilities between the Soviet Union and the United States, Powers replied, "The people who sent me should think of these things. My job was to carry out orders. I do not think it was my responsibility to make such decisions." When asked why he did it, he answered, "I was ordered to."[5] It was a soldier's straightforward, unequivocal approach to duty, one which, at an earlier period of history would have been accepted without question as legitimate as it was honest. It was, in fact, the position taken by almost all the defendants at Nuremberg at the end of World War II. Adolf Eichmann used the same plea of *respondeat superior* when he was brought to trial in Israel; he did, however, recognize that he was guilty of moral cowardice, since morality demanded that he disobey his superior orders.[6]

For many years it was an accepted principle that military orders should demand and receive absolute and unqualified obedience. Unquestioned dedication was deemed necessary in order to preserve discipline and to assure efficiency and despatch. How could any military force operate effectively if it could not rely upon the complete

---

[4] Ibid., p. 145.
[5] The questions were put to Powers by the presiding judge, Lieut.-Gen. Viktor Borisoglebsky. *New York Times*, August 19, 1960, p. 8, col. 4.
[6] Mackenzie, *On Moral Courage*, p. 245.

subordination of the individual's will to that of the commander of the armed forces of which the individual was a member, and the state of which he was the servant?[7] After all, the state was the master. It was the soldier's duty to obey his superiors, military and political, not to impose his views upon them. It was the Bushido code. Without knowing it as such, that was how Gary Powers saw it.

Until 1749 English law postulated the binding quality of military orders.[8] In that year, however, limits were imposed upon the military code of absolute obedience. Henceforth obedience was to be confined to *lawful* orders only. This qualification has remained an essential part of English military law ever since. A "lawful" order, however, was not defined. What was "lawful" and what was "unlawful" remained an open question. The British, with their peculiar genius for flexibility in law and their skill at avoiding definitions, left the question to be decided by the courts. Here are some examples of what was done. In 1816, one Thomas, a sentinel on a British warship, was ordered to keep small boats away from the vessel while the ship's crew was being paid off. After issuing several warnings to approaching boats only to find that his warnings were ignored, Thomas fired his musket, killing an occupant of one of the boats. He was charged with murder. The jury believed that the defendant had acted under the honest impression that it was his duty to fire; but the judges convicted him, at the same time stating that his was, however, a case deserving pardon.[9] Another leading case was that of *Regina v. Smith*, 1900. During the Boer War, a British patrol encountered a stupid or recalcitrant native who refused to aid the patrol. One of the soldiers, acting upon the orders of his superior officer, shot the native. Smith, the soldier in question, was acquitted by the court, although in a way which left room for conviction in other cases.[10] In both instances, it will be noted, the court, while adhering to the letter of the law, was disposed to look sympathetically upon the defendant.

In Canada we have followed British practice and precedent, pretty much to the letter. The various Militia Acts adopted after 1868 contained no statement of military law peculiar to this country; they simply, by reference, incorporated the Army Act of the United Kingdom into Canadian law, thus making it a Canadian statute. British military law was accepted without question, although from time to time, minor modifications were introduced to meet particular Cana-

---

[7] S. P. Huntingdon, *The Soldier and the State* (Cambridge, 1964), pp. 16, 57-58, 73.

[8] Guenter Lewy, "Superior Orders, Nuclear Warfare, and the Dictates of Conscience," *The American Political Science Review*, vol. 55, no. 1 (March 1961), p. 6.

[9] Sheldon Glueck, *War Criminals: Their Prosecution and Punishment* (New York, 1944), n. 31, pp. 239-40.

[10] Ibid., pp. 149.

dian conditions and attitudes. Not until 1950, when the Canadian Parliament adopted the National Defence Act, did Canadians produce their own military law, in the form of the Code of Military Service Discipline, which was appended to the Act.[11] The Code emphasized the fact that in Canada a soldier was a citizen and, as such, was amenable to all laws applying to Canadian citizens, civilian or military. It also emphasized the fact that the Code of Discipline in no way altered the power of the civil courts to try any member of the armed services for an offence triable by the courts in the case of civilians. This did not mean that the military courts were thus deprived of their traditional roles. On the contrary, the Act listed the offences which could be tried by the various courts-martial (general court-martial and disciplinary courts-martial) including the familiar charge of disobedience of a *lawful* command.[12]

The Americans, too, tended to follow British precedent, although not quite so literally as the Canadians. They, too, accepted the principle of obedience to *lawful* orders and left the definition to the courts. The most notable American case was that of *The United States v. Jones*, 1813.[13] This was a case involving the crew of an American privateer which, under the orders of their captain, boarded a Portuguese vessel on the high seas, assaulted the Portuguese captain, and stole a number of items from his ship. Handing down the decision, the presiding judge stated that any doctrine to the effect that a military or civil officer could command an inferior to violate the laws of the United States was "alarming and unfounded . . .repugnant to reason, and to the positive law of the land." The *Jones* case made it clear that a subordinate could not plead superior orders as a defence for any action he actually knew to be illegal; neither could he plead ignorance when the circumstances were such that an average man could not help but realize that the action ordered was illegal. This decision was given added strength by a subsequent supreme court case, *Mitchell v. Harmony*, 1851, in which the chief justice stated that a military officer could not plead in defence of an

---

[11] National Defence Act, 14 George VI C43, assented to June 30, 1950, *Statutes of Canada* (Ottawa, 1950), vol. 1.

[12] Ibid., sec. 62 (1). Introducing the Bill in the Canadian Parliament, Minister of National Defence Brooke Claxton said, "Experience gained during the last war showed clearly the need for more unified control and greater uniformity in the three services. Further, the present position and status of Canada made it undesirable to depend for the discipline of our army and air force upon legislation enacted by a legislative body not responsible to the people of Canada. Accordingly, soon after becoming minister, I directed that work be commenced on the preparation of a single, all-embracing Canadian statute to include a common disciplinary code applicable to all three services." *Debates of the House of Commons*, Canada, vol. 111, May 16, 1950, p. 2538.

[13] 26 *Fed. Cas.*, pp. 653, 657-58, no. 15, 494 (C.C.D., Pa. 1813). See Glueck, *War Criminals*, pp. 146.

unlawful act that he did it under the order of a superior. The order might palliate, the judge suggested, but it could never justify.[14]

The German position was not greatly dissimilar. Ever since 1872, the German Military Penal Code had been specific in its rejection of the plea of superior orders as a defence for what would otherwise be an illegal act. In 1921 the German Supreme Court relied upon this rule in the case of the German submariners who machine-gunned the survivors of the Canadian Hospital Ship *Llandovery Castle*, on June 27, 1918.[15] The defendants pleaded the orders of their superior officer, but the presiding judge remarked that they "should . . . have refused to obey. As they did not do so, they must be punished." He added, moreover, that the action of the submariners was contrary to the international law of war: "The rule of international law, which is here involved, is simple and is universally known. No possible doubt can exist with regard to the question of its applicability. The court must in this instance affirm Patzig's guilt of killing contrary to international law."[16]

The introduction of international law into this case and its application to individuals was an innovation. Nothing like this had been done before; and it constituted a precedent neither Great Britain nor the United States was in any hurry to adopt. Despite the adherence of both nations to the various Hague Conventions, the 1914 edition of the British *Manual of Military Law* stated categorically: "Members of armed forces who commit such violations of the recognized rules of warfare as are ordered by their government or by their commander, are not war criminals and cannot therefore be punished by the enemy."[17] The

---

[14] 13 Howard (1851), pp. 115, 137. See ibid., pp. 147, 238.

[15] G. W. L. Nicholson, *Canada's Nursing Sisters* (Toronto, 1975), pp. 94-96.

[16] Glueck, *War Criminals*, p. 152; Lewy, "Superior Orders," p. 7.

[17] *Manual of Military Law* (1914), art. 443. Quoted in Glueck, *War Criminals*, p. 150. A case of particular Canadian interest was that brought against a Canadian, Alexander McLeod, by a New York court, in 1840. McLeod was one of the Canadians who, acting under the orders of Col. Allan McNab, crossed the Niagara River, December 29, 1827, into the United States, seized and burned the vessel *Caroline* which was being used to carry supplies to W. L. Mackenzie's insurgents on Navy Island. In the course of action an American citizen was killed. In 1840 McLeod was arrested and charged with murder. The British minister in Washington demanded McLeod's release, on the grounds that the destruction of the *Caroline* was "a public act" carried out "by persons in Her Majesty's service, obeying the orders of the superior authorities." The act, therefore, "according to the usages of nations, can only be the subject of discussion between two national governments. It cannot justly be made the ground of legal proceedings in the United States, against the individuals concerned, who were bound to obey the authorities appointed by their own government." McLeod was, however, tried and acquitted. The United States Secretary of State, however, admitted that the British position was valid. W. E. Hall, in his *Treatise on International Law*, 5th ed. (Oxford, 1904), p. 314, agreed with the Secretary of State. He wrote, "When a state in the exercise of its right of self-preservation does acts of violence, within the territory of a foreign state, while remaining at peace with it, its agents

American military code said much the same thing. In 1914, paragraph 347 of the *Rules of Land Warfare* laid down that "individuals of the armed forces will not be punished for these offences [against the laws of war] in case they are committed under the orders or sanction of their government or commanders."[18] Both the British and American positions, as stated above, remained unchanged until 1944, when both countries, in anticipation of an Allied military victory and the possibility of conducting the trials of enemy "war criminals," and anxious to preserve their virtue, reversed their positions and agreed that

> The fact that a rule of warfare has been violated in pursuance of an order of the belligerent Government or of an individual belligerent commander does not deprive the act in question of its character as a war crime . . . members of the armed forces are bound to obey lawful orders only and . . . cannot therefore escape liability if, in obedience to a command, they commit acts which both violate unchallenged rules of warfare and outrage the general sentiment of humanity. . . .[19]

The Germans had no need to perform such a flip-flop. They had already accepted the doctrine that offences contrary to international law could be tried before the courts. Article 4 of the Weimar constitution provided that "the generally accepted rules of International Law are to be considered as binding integral parts of the law of the German Reich."[20] Apparently not suspecting that his own words could be used against him, Joseph Goebbels took to the press to denounce Allied air raids as "terror bombing" and a violation of international law. The airmen, if caught, could not find shelter behind the formula of orders from their political and military superiors. "It is not provided in any military law," he wrote indignantly in the *Volkischer Beobachter*, that the perpetrator of "a despicable crime" was "exempt from punishment because he blames his superior, especially if the orders of the latter are in evident contradiction to all human morality and every international usage of warfare."[21]

By the end of World War II, it was widely agreed in international circles that *respondeat superior* was no longer acceptable as a defence for questionable actions committed during a time of hostilities, regardless of what the historical precedents might be, and that international law could be invoked in the case of alleged war crimes. This is obvious from

---

cannot be tried for the murder of persons killed by them, nor are they liable in civil action in respect of damage to property which they may have caused."

[18] *Rules of Land Warfare*, Field Manual 27-10, Washington, 1940, art. 347. See also Glueck, *War Criminals*, p. 140.

[19] *History of the United Nations War Crimes Commission and the Development of the Laws of War* (London, 1948), p. 282.

[20] R. H. Jackson, *The Nuremberg Case* (New York, 1947), p. 84.

[21] *Volkischer Beobachter*, May 28-29, 1944, quoted in Lewy, "Superior Orders," p. 7.

the charter of the International Military Tribunal: "The fact that the Defendant acted pursuant to order of his Government or of a superior, shall not free him from responsibility, but may be considered in mitigation of punishment, if the Tribunal determine that justice so requires."[22] All the soldiers and politicians tried at Nuremberg were tried pursuant to this principle. It must be admitted, however, that not much respect was accorded the argument that superior orders should be considered "in mitigation of punishment."

The old doctrine of absolute obedience to superior orders is now pretty much discredited. The only plea that may be advanced with any possibility of a sympathetic hearing is that the defendant acted under duress, and perhaps that he acted in ignorance of the illegality of his action, no wrongful intent being present in his mind. "The obedience of a soldier is not the obedience of an automaton," declared the Nuremberg tribunal. "A soldier is a reasoning agent. He does not respond, and is not expected to respond like a piece of machinery.... To plead superior orders one must show an excusable ignorance of their illegality."[23]

The new doctrine, to all intents and purposes, may now be considered an integral part of the international law governing the conduct of war. Just how widely the nations of the world accepted this development will be appreciated after a glance at the following quotations. The first is taken from the 1958 edition of the British *Law of War on Land*: "Obedience to the order of a government or of a superior, whether military or civil, or to a national law or regulation, affords no defence to a charge of committing a war crime, but may be considered in mitigation."[24] An explanatory note, however, makes it clear that in the case of senior military commanders, no such mitigating factor will be taken into account. The second quotation is taken from the *Basic Law of the German Federal Republic*, article 25: "The general rules of international law shall form part of federal law. They shall take precedence over the laws and create rights and duties directly for the inhabitants of the federal territory."[25] The same article adds that if an inferior refuses to

---

[22] *Trial of the Major War Criminals Before the International Military Tribunal 14 November 1945-1 October 1946*, Official Text in the English Language (Nuremberg, 1947), art. 8, vol. 1, p. 12. For a discussion of *respondeat superior* see Yoram Dinstein, "The Defense of Obedience to Superior Orders," *International Law* (Leyden, 1965).

[23] *Ignorantia legis non excusat* has long been a principle of civil law. But the Nuremberg tribunal was not prepared to reject outright the possibility that the illegality of certain actions might not have been understood or appreciated by those of inferior rank, and that in such instances, no wrongful intent was present. *Trials of War Criminals Before the Nuremberg Military Tribunals under Control Council Law, No. 10, October 1946 to April 1949*, vol. 4 (Washington, 1950), pp. 470, 473. See also Lewy, "Superior Orders," p. 8.

[24] *British Law of War (1958)*, art. 627, p. 176. See Lewy, "Superior Orders," p. 9.

[25] H. W. Briggs, *The Law of Nations* (New York, 1952), p. 58. See also Lewy, "Superior Orders," p. 10.

carry out an order violating human dignity, he is not guilty of insubordination. In fact, no order is to be executed "if obedience to it would constitute a crime or transgression." The military law of the Union of Soviet Socialist Republics (USSR) is somewhat less idealistic. It posits strict obedience to orders, but concedes "the right to make complaints about illegal actions and orders of commanders." It also states that a soldier carrying out the unlawful order of a superior "incurs no responsibility for the crime, which is that of the officer, except where the soldier fulfils an order which is clearly criminal, in which case the soldier is responsible with the officer who issued the order."[26]

3

To THE jurist, the question of obedience is fundamentally one of obedience to whom? To a superior officer? A national government? A supra-national body such as the United Nations? To the philosopher the question of obedience is approached as obedience to what? To law, of course; but what law? Positive law or natural law? The law of the state or the law of God?

Man is a social and political animal. Because he does not exist in isolation, how he achieved the socio-political organization we now call the state has been the subject of many theories. Thomas Hobbes suggested that human individuals came together because of inability to cope with the violence of the natural state; that the motivation behind the state was thus one of self-preservation. Jean Jacques Rousseau preferred to think of the state as the product of a social contract. Others have portrayed the state as today's stage in the evolution of the individual through the family and the kin-group or clan to the national state, with its special institutions embodying authority and hierarchy. The state is not necessarily the ultimate in socio-political organization. For the moment, however, the state is the basic instrument of our political and social life. The state is, therefore, a product of the human will. It exists because we will it to exist. This will is revealed in our loyalty towards the state and in our willingness to accept its decisions, regulations, and laws. This does not mean, cannot mean, that every individual citizen must necessarily give his or her personal approbation to every law of the state. Such unanimity is simply not feasible. To insist upon it would be to promote stagnation or even chaos. And so we, as citizens, obey the laws of the state, not because these laws are always right but because we consider that it is right to obey the law.[27] All law takes on the

---

[26] Morris Greenspan, *The Modern Law of Land Warfare* (Berkeley, 1959), p. 491.

[27] R. M. MacIver, *The Modern State* (London, 1926), p. 154. MacIver wrote, "Political obligation is based on the general recognition of the universal service of law and

form of an imperative, and it is for that reason that the state takes cognizance of refusals to obey the law. And we, as citizens, because we do not wish to return to a violent state of nature, to violate the social contract, or to look back over the long path of evolution, are willing to accept the idea that the state may legitimately use force to prevent the rule of force, and use law to maintain the rule of law. At the same time, we realize that the state, if it is wise, will avoid straining the citizen's sense of law-abidingness, by avoiding the imposition of such rules, regulations, or laws as may be resented by a large portion of the citizen body. For, when loyalty disintegrates, obedience becomes a matter of coercion rather than of conscience; that is to say, the imperative of the positive law becomes wholly separated from the imperative of natural law.

For some 2,000 years the concept of natural law has been a recurring motif in Western political thought. Natural law is not, of course, a written code making it possible for every human being to determine *a priori* human behaviour; it is an indication of what is good as against what is evil in the hearts and minds of men. It is a pronouncement on the values of human action. According to Jacques Maritain, natural law, as applied to man, is virtually coexistent with the whole field of natural morality.[28] Natural law, like human conscience, is part of the progressive growth of man. It is the product of his reason, his experience, his drive to achieve fullness of being and his search for the truth. Its vitality and durability could not help but place it in apposition and sometimes in opposition to positive law (i.e., written, man-made law). The question that arises is: which law should take priority in men's thoughts and hearts, natural law or positive law? Which law should provide the guidelines for conduct?

According to the Greek philosopher, Socrates, the answer was simple enough. In any conflict between the state and god (and by god he meant perfect good, perfect justice) god must take priority; in any conflict between man (and by man he meant human self-interest) and the state, the state should prevail. And Socrates answered the question by forfeiting his life. He refused to obey the injunction of the state to cease teaching; but, at the same time, when offered the opportunity to escape from Athens, he declined to do so. He was prepared to accept punishment. In this way he put god above the state, but placed the state above himself. He would not answer evil with evil. The state must be

government, for the sake of which we accept specific enactments, which in themselves we disapprove. This is the principle of the general will, and all our acquired traditions of loyalty include the assumption that we should extend our law-abidingness beyond the limits of immediate approbation."

[28] N. W. Michener, *Maritain on the Nature of Man in a Christian Democracy* (Hull, 1955), p. 71.

dissuaded but not disobeyed.[29] Jesus of Nazareth, like Socrates, could have escaped death; but in refusing to give up his mission, he accepted the penalty imposed by Judaic law. "Not my will, but thine, be done."[30]

In Rome Cicero adopted much the same approach when he wrote in his *de Republica*:

> True law is right reason in agreement with Nature; it is of universal application, unchanging and everlasting; it summons to duty by its commands and averts from wrong-doing by its prohibitions. . . . We cannot be freed from its obligations by Senate or People, and we need not look outside ourselves for an expounder or interpreter of it. And there will not be different laws at Rome and at Athens, or different laws now and in the future, but one eternal and unchangeable law will be valid for all nations and for all times. . . .[31]

The doctrine of natural law expressed in this passage was incorporated in the writings of the Roman jurists and grafted to the teachings of the Christian church. Together jurists and theologians provided the material out of which Justinian, the Christian law-giver of Rome, fashioned his *Corpus Juris Civilis*, a book which, after the Bible, left the greatest impression upon the history of western Europe. Writing in 1670 to the English philosopher, Thomas Hobbes, the German, Gottfried Leibniz, remarked that in his effort to reduce Roman law to its elements, he found that half of it was "pure natural law."[32]

In its essence, natural law is a matter of morality. It is not only a measure of action but a pronouncement on the value of that action. Good and evil become conditions of obligation. Hugo Grotius, the Dutch jurist, saw the law of nature as "a dictate of right reason which points out that an act . . . has in it the quality of moral baseness or moral necessity," a definition which would have met with the approval of St. Thomas Aquinas.[33] But while the writings of Aquinas had a religious

---

[29] See selections from "The Apology of Socrates" and "Crito," in Curtis Crawford, *Civil Disobedience: A Casebook* (New York, 1973), pp. 2-31.

[30] The Gospel According to Saint Luke 22:42.

[31] M. Tulli Ciceronis, *Opera Omnia*, ed. by C. F. A. Nobbe (Lipsiae, 1849), vol. 9, De Republica Lib. III, xxii, 33,16, p. 325. "Est quidem vera lex recta ratio, naturae congruens, diffusa in omnes, constans, sempiterna, quae vocet ad officium iubendo, netando a fraude deterreat . . . nec vero aut per senatum aut per populum solvi hac lege possumus: neque est quaerendus explanator aut interpres euis alius: nec erit alia lex Romae, alia Athenis, alia nunc, alia posthac; sed et mones gentes et omni tempori una lex et sempiterna et immutabilis contenebit, unusque erit communis quasi magister et imperator omnium deus. . . ."

[32] A. P. d'Entrèves, *Natural Law: An Introduction to Legal Philosophy* (London, 1951), p. 32. The very perfection of the Roman system of laws led to its veneration as the embodiment of natural justice.

[33] Quoted in ibid. St. Thomas Aquinas wrote, "The rational creature is subject to Divine providence in the most excellent way; in so far as it partakes of a share of providence, by being provident both for itself and for others. Wherefore it has a share of

bent to them, those of Grotius, Puffendorf, and Vattel, writing in the seventeenth and eighteenth centuries, are of secular inspiration. And it is this secular quality which has given natural law the strength which it has enjoyed since.

During the nineteenth and twentieth centuries efforts have been made to reduce natural law to some kind of a written code, at least as far as the relations of national states with one another are concerned. I need only refer to the international gatherings at Geneva and at the Hague. Natural law was the inspiration behind the efforts to "humanize" warfare, if I may use that term, by prohibiting the use of those weapons, arms, projectiles, or other means calculated to cause unnecessary suffering, and by laying down rules for the humane treatment of prisoners of war and noncombatants. When a special commission was set up after World War I to look into breaches of international law, the members were required to investigate not only breaches of "explicit regulations," that is, positive law, but also of "established customs" and "the clear dictates of humanity," in other words, breaches of the natural law.[34] Under article 227 of the Treaty of Versailles, William II, formerly Emperor of Germany, was to be called to account for "the supreme offence against international morality and the sanctity of treaties."[35] The government of the Netherlands, under whose protection William II had placed himself, refused, however, to turn him over to the Allied powers. The Dutch took a purely legalistic stand: "The Government of the Queen cannot admit in the present case any other duty than that imposed on it by the laws of the kingdom and national tradition"; and obviously the charges against the German Emperor were not those listed in any of the categories to be found in the extradition treaties the Netherlands had negotiated with the powers concerned.[36] To have used coercion against the Netherlands would have been a breach of that very morality to which the Allies were paying lip service, and so William II remained in Doorn chopping wood and writing his memoirs.

The Treaty of Versailles also called for the arrest of several hundred alleged war criminals, among whom were to be found the

---

the Eternal Reason, whereby it has a natural inclination to its proper act and end: and this participation of the eternal law in the rational creature is called the Natural Law." St. Thomas Aquinas, *Summa Theologica*, trans. by the Fathers of the English Dominican Province (New York, 1947), vol. 1, Treatise on Law, question 91, art. 2, p. 997. For a brief summary of the ideas of Grotius in relation to natural law, war, and peace, see W. S. M. Knight, *Hugonis Grotii de Jure Belli ac Pacis Libri Tres Selections*, The Grotius Society Publications, 3 (London, 1922). (See Prolegomena and Book 1 in particular.)

[34] Quoted in Glueck, *War Criminals*, p. 19.

[35] The punitive clauses of the Treaty of Versailles included 227, 228, 229, and 230.

[36] "Punishing War Criminals: Allies and the Ex-Kaiser," *Current History*, vol. 11, part 2 (March 1920), p. 377.

former German Chancellor von Bethmann-Holweg, General von Hindenburg, and Admirals von Tirpitz and Scheer. The new republican government of Germany was, however, reluctant to carry out its obligations under the treaty. And because the Allied powers were disinclined to use force to back up demands that were without historical precedent and charges which were, in many instances, incapable of proof under the standards laid down for use in British courts, little was done to proceed with the war trials. In the end twelve charges were laid and six alleged war criminals, including those involved in the case of the *Llandovery Castle*, were tried by German courts.[37]

The war trials after World War II were a different matter. The politicians, generals, and admirals who sat in the dock at Nuremberg, were found guilty not only of breaches of the positive aspects of international law but also of actions that were "inherently criminal and contrary to the accepted principles of humanity as recognized and accepted by civilized nations."[38] What did these words mean if not natural law as conceived by the philosophers and theologians of the past centuries? The principles of humanity! The same words had been used in the preamble of the Hague Convention; and when they were repeated in the Krupp trial, the tribunal expressly stated that they implied "much more than a pious declaration"; that they were, in fact, "the legal yardstick to be applied if and when the specific conventional provisions of the Convention and the regulations annexed to it do not cover specific cases occurring in warfare."[39] The words used by the court were vague and subjective. They were, as one jurist put it, "liable to alter with the passing years," and as another remarked, "an unchartable area of discretion."[40] Perhaps they would have been better served had they been applied to those on the winning side as well as those on the losing side.[41] Was Goering being prophetic when, after listening to the indictment, he remarked, "The victor will always be the judge and the vanquished, the accused"?[42] Nevertheless, imperfect as the Nuremberg trials may have been, they established the principles of

---

[37] The so-called "book of hate," i.e., the list of those persons demanded by the Allied powers to be brought to trial, included almost 900 names. See ibid., p. 373.

[38] *Trials of War Criminals*, vol. 11, p. 543.

[39] Ibid., p. 1341. See also Lewy, "Superior Orders," p. 16.

[40] P. E. Corbett, *Law and Society in the Relations of States* (New York, 1951), p. 268.

[41] What may be said of the British order in early 1942 that bombing targets were *not* to be military or industrial targets: "The aiming points are to be built-up areas, not for instance, the dockyards or aircraft factories." N. Frankland, *Bomber Offensive: The Demolition of Europe* (New York, 1970), pp. 24ff. See also C. P. Snow, *Science and Government* (Cambridge, 1961).

[42] Quoted by Lewy, "Superior Orders," p. 17. James Marshall, in *Swords and Symbols* (New York, 1969), p. 206, says that the "law" applied at Nuremberg was "the law of the triumphant."

natural law, the principles of humanity, if you prefer, as a legitimate standard by which to measure international criminality in the future.

But the Nuremberg precedent has certain implications which must be considered. Where would President Harry Truman, who authorized the use of the atomic bomb against Hiroshima and Nagasaki, and the airmen who delivered the bombs, stand in any trial where natural law or the laws of humanity provided the standard of judgment? Since they were not tried, no court was ever called upon to express an opinion. But we must remember that the present-day military codes of Germany, Great Britain, and the United States (and by the same token, Canada) affirm the validity of the principles of "humanity and chivalry" in warfare. What would be the position of any politician or soldier in a future war in which atomic weapons and other even more fearful products of military technology will be available, and in all probability, used? Consider the soldier's predicament. Should he refuse to obey his superiors, who are often far from the scenes of carnage and destruction, and risk court-martial and punishment; or should he suppress his moral scruples, obey his orders, and risk being held accountable by a war crimes tribunal (if he happens to be on the losing side)? That was the dilemma which faced Field Marshal Wilhelm Keitel, Chief of the *Oberkommando der Wehrmacht*, or Supreme Command of the Armed Forces. Keitel received his orders directly from Hitler and carried them out. "As a German soldier by inclination and conviction," he told the court at Nuremberg, "I believe it my duty to take full responsibility for what I have done, even if it should have been wrong." "But you are not only a soldier," replied his counsel. "You are a personality with a life and conscience of our own. You must have had thoughts when an action you might have thought was unjust, was planned." "I grew up in a traditional military environment and we were not concerned with right or wrong," was the answer.[43] It was rather like that of Gary Powers.

The possibility of British soldiers in the same predicament was debated in the British House of Lords in 1950 and 1952. The question under discussion concerned the use of the atomic bomb against an enemy. Should an airman ordered to deliver the bomb do so without any questions of conscience? Should he run the risk of being shot or hanged by a victorious tribunal dealing with acts violating the principles of humanity? Lord Chatfield somewhat cynically asked whether there were any "general sentiments of humanity." One noble earl asked, "Do we tell the air crews who carry and deliver an atomic bomb not to outrage the general sentiments of humanity? Do we hold that one of the air crew, if captured, ought not to be treated by the enemy as a war criminal?" Would not every airman who took part in what the

---

[43] R. W. Cooper, *The Nuremberg Trials* (Baltimore, 1947), p. 231.

victors would unquestionably call a "war of aggression" be regarded as a war criminal? Another noble lord maintained, as Field Marshal Keitel had done, that soldiers should execute their orders without misgivings about the legality of their orders under international law.[44] Any other rule would simply undermine military discipline and hamper military efficiency.

What is the answer to this agonizing dilemma? Perhaps there is no answer. But the dilemma is there and will remain. And the soldier must give the response that Home gave, or the one given by Keitel. Perhaps all that can be said at this point is that those who choose a military career have either to satisfy themselves that they have no moral obligation but to do their military duty, or to contract out.[45]

4

NOT ONLY did natural law, as I have pointed out earlier, tend to become secularized in the form of international law during the eighteenth and nineteenth centuries; it also tended to become politicized. This process of politicization was the outcome of a shift in the emphasis from natural law to natural rights. There is a difference. A law is the expression of the will of a ruler, a governing council or a parliament; a right is the assertion on the part of an individual (or group of individuals) of his power to act for his own good on the basis of right reason, or natural law.[46] The exercise of rights, therefore, supposes a rational being and a concept of common good; natural rights are predicated upon natural law. The latter provides the vindication of the former.

The man who gave impetus to the discussion of natural rights was the English philosopher, John Locke. The influence of Locke, and also of Thomas Paine, but principally of Locke, is apparent in the American Declaration of Independence, 1776, and of the French *Déclaration des Droits de l'Homme*, 1789. The Americans wrote about natural rights as "self-evident truths" which included equality, life, liberty, and the pursuit of happiness for all citizens, and the alteration or abolition of any government which appeared "destructive of these ends." Frenchmen declared that "ignorance, oblivion or contempt of the rights of man" were the "only causes of public misfortune and of the corruption of governments." They saw it as their duty to make

---

[44] *House of Lords Debates*, July 19, 1950; May 14, 1952. Quoted in Lewy, "Superior Orders," p. 5.

[45] See M. Cohen, T. Nagel, and T. Scanlon (eds.), *War and Moral Responsibility* (Princeton, 1974), for a discussion examining the ethical and legal restrictions on military methods and aims. These essays, it should be remarked, were written in the light of the American experience in Vietnam. One of the contributors, however, does raise the argument of "military necessity" as a justification for actions that might otherwise be regarded as immoral (S. Levinson, "Responsibility for Crimes of War," pp. 104-37).

[46] T. H. Green, *Lectures on the Principles of Political Obligation* (Oxford, 1927), p. 207.

people aware of "the natural, inalienable, and sacred rights of man" beginning with the assertion that all men were "born free and remain free and equal in rights." Briefly they argued that one man's opinion was as valid as another's, and one man's vote was as significant as another's. In practical terms this meant liberal democracy, with its concepts of popular sovereignty and its representative institutions. But it also could be interpreted, and was interpreted, as an incitement to rebellion against authority in the name of the rights of man, of freedom, and of liberation. It is hardly surprising, is it, that the nineteenth century was the century of rebellions, revolutions, and wars of liberation? Hence the overthrow of Charles X and Louis Philippe and the popular election of Louis Napoleon as president in France; hence the Carlist wars in Spain; hence the events of 1848 in Germany; hence the rebellions of William Lyon Mackenzie and Louis Joseph Papineau in Canada.

The problems of loyalty and obedience imposed upon men during the nineteenth century as a result of the spread of doctrines of political liberalism and natural rights, are as pressing today as they were in the earlier period. Perhaps even more pressing, as natural rights, which concentrated upon extending popular representation in the institutions of government in the earlier period, now reach out to other fields of public endeavour. No longer are natural rights considered merely as political rights, but also as economic, linguistic, ethnic, and cultural in character. Emphasis is now placed upon the alleged rights of the individual as against the rights of the community, of the state. Today we seem to be living in a period of intellectual as well as political confusion, as anarchism, collectivism, communism, and nationalism, all in the name of human rights, contend for men's loyalties and their obedience. Obedience, not to whom, but to what? Rousseau's *volonté générale*? No longer is that enough. The divine right of kings yields to the divine right to oppose kings. Opposition to the *status quo*, whatever form it may take, has become the ultimate righteousness. At least in the eyes of the dissenter.

As far as I am concerned personally, I find it difficult to concede that dissent can legitimately claim a prior guarantee that in any given case it is right and just, and that the dissenter's judgment, as against that of the so-called establishment, is necessarily inspired by right reason. Is dissent *qua* dissent really the *Vox Dei*? To my mind, to seek to achieve political, economic, or cultural aims by force is stupid; for force is the poorest servant of intelligence. Better by far to count heads than to break them.

What I am saying is that the validity of resistance to and disobedience of the commands of the state depends, in the final analysis, upon the motivation behind that resistance and disobedience. If the motivation is irrational egotism, eccentricity, or self-interest, social, political, or economic, then disobedience is fundamentally immoral. I frankly admit that it is hard to assess the quality of motivation. But I suspect that human motives are not always devoid of moral depravity and that ambition and cultural or national vanity not infrequently masquerade as selflessness. That is why I am prepared to give the benefit of doubt to the state and to the law; because I accept the possibility of an innate sense of justice in most people, without which they would not be willing to enforce the law or defend its position. In brief, I accept "a presumption in favour of compliance in the absence of good reason to the contrary."[47] That is why, with Socrates, I am ready, in the ordinary course of events, to obey the commands of the state.

But with Socrates' qualifications. I admit that when norms and values clearly diverge, disobedience is morally justified, remembering always that such disobedience must be addressed clearly to the sense of justice of the majority. Disobedience should be limited to what is unquestionably an injustice which, if rectified, would establish a basis for a return to obedience. An obviously immoral law presents a dilemma to the citizen; an immoral command presents a dilemma to the soldier. In each case the individual concerned must and will act in the way his moral principles demand. He cannot do otherwise. And he will take the responsibility for his action, knowing full well that only the thin line of fate separates the hero from the villain and the patriot from the rebel. John Churchill's disloyalty took him to a dukedom; Simon Fraser's took him to the block. Arnold's fate was lasting opprobrium, and Andrei Vlasov's was death. So too was Louis Riel's. And we all know the fate of the generals of Iran's Imperial Guard, who remained loyal to the Shah. The paths of loyalty lead to the grave as frequently as those of disloyalty lead to glory. It all depends upon loyalty to whom and to what.

5

I BEGAN this discussion of the problems of loyalty with a brief account of the experience of a British soldier's disobedience in World War II. I shall end it with an account of a French soldier's disobedience in Algeria. Both experiences involve moral courage and the moral dilemma of loyalty.

Pierre Alexandre Joseph Chateau-Jobert was one of France's best-known paratroop commanders and most decorated soldiers. Escaping to England after the capitulation of France in 1940, he joined the Forces Françaises Libre (F.F.L.) under de Gaulle, and, at the end of August, was sent to Africa with the 13e demi-brigade de Légion Etrangère under the name of Captain Conan, a pseudonym taken to protect

---

[47] John Rawls, "The Justification of Civil Disobedience," in James Rachels (ed.), *Moral Problems: A Collection of Philosophical Essays* (New York, 1971), p. 193.

his family from reprisals. After serving in Eritrea, Syria, and Libya, he returned to England in 1943 to undergo training as a paratrooper. Given command of the 3rd French Special Air Service (S.A.S.) Regiment, he parachuted into France on several occasions to assist the French *Résistance*, and in 1944 landed in France with de Gaulle's Free French. After the war he remained in the French army and undertook to organize paratroop schools at Lannion and Pau-Idron. Subsequently he spent several years in Indo-China, between 1947 and 1952, in command of a demi-brigade of "commandos-parachutistes." After a brief sojourn in Algeria, he joined the Anglo-French expedition against Egypt in 1956, leading his 2ᵉ Régiment de Parachutistes Coloniaux in the drop on Port Said.

During World War II, Chateau-Jobert gave no thought to the moral aspects of what he was doing. After all, what could take priority over the liberation of one's own country? In Indo-China, however, he began to ask himself disturbing questions. What was the purpose of the war in the east? Why were French troops burning villages and inflicting hardships, even tortures, on the local people? To maintain the French presence and French influence in Indo-China was the answer. But why? What superior moral values did French culture possess that it should be forced upon the inhabitants of far eastern Asia? Were the precepts of Christ very much different from those of Buddha or Confucius? Finally, Jobert came to the conclusion that there were certain basic values which should govern human conduct; principles that were universally acceptable to all men, whether they were French or Vietnamese: justice; charity, in the sense of love of one's neighbour; consideration for the rights of others; respect for human dignity.[48] Simple virtues, all of them, but too frequently missing from the politics of democratic and communist countries alike. From what Jobert could see, the universally accepted political principle was that the end justified the means. And that meant the ready acceptance of inadmissible or immoral means, hypocrisy, and deceit. "J'étais en train de découvrir," he wrote, "le bluff des hommes politiques qui, une fois au pouvoir, font passer d'abominables agissements sur la *raison d'état*, pour se donner une justification de bafouer certains principes de simple morale."[49] He was further disturbed by the events of Port Said, not by the actual operation itself but by the rationale behind it. As a paratroop exercise, it had been a success; but politically it was a failure. Some of the participants cynically called it "Un coup pour le brevet, un coup pour les décorations."[50]

---

[48] P. A. J. Chateau-Jobert, *Feux et Lumière sur ma Trace* (Paris, 1978), p. 114. These were the essence of natural law.

[49] Ibid., pp. 148-49.

[50] Ibid., p. 202.

After Egypt, Chateau-Jobert and his paratroops returned to Algeria. Here they found themselves hard pressed to cope with the terrorist tactics adopted by the Front de Libération Nationale (F.L.N.), particularly when confronted with the indecisiveness and lack of purpose of a French government which was playing hot and cold with the Algerian-born whites and the native Algerians who supported the French cause. They wondered if Algeria would be another Indo-China, and if, in the end, French politicians would betray both the army and the people of Algeria. As the Algerian struggle continued into the 1960s it took on, more and more, as far as Chateau-Jobert was concerned, the aspect of a moral issue: a contest between loyalty and disloyalty, hypocrisy and truth, betrayal and good faith. With the full support of the government the paratroopers believed that they could win; without it they were simply throwing away their lives.

Thus, when General de Gaulle, who had been the soul and inspiration of the French resistance to the Germans, assured the army and the people of France that he would never abandon French Algeria, they believed him. And when he did just that, he betrayed the trust they had placed in him, and became an impostor, no better than the corrupt politicians who placed political expediency higher than honour.[51] What were the soldiers in Algeria to do; what were the pro-French Algerians to do? That was the problem with which many of them, including Chateau-Jobert, were faced. Were they bound by an oath of loyalty to the man who, in their eyes, had become a traitor; or were they bound by their lively sense of loyalty to a France which de Gaulle had ceased to personify? As far as the commander of the 2^e R.P.C. was concerned, his duty was to France—the ideal which he had served in Europe, Africa, Indo-China, Egypt, and Algeria. To him it was a matter of conscience as against the law; and conscience was the stronger. That is why Pierre Chateau-Jobert, the Breton who had studied at the Centre des Hautes Etudes Militaires, the "école des maréchaux," chose to abandon a career that would have taken him to a high command and threw in his lot with Raoul Salan and the Organisation Armée Secrète (O.A.S.).

Chateau-Jobert knew what his fate would be should the O.A.S. fail: a firing squad or self-imposed exile. As he expected, he was tried *in absentia* and sentenced to death. And for seven years he remained a hunted figure in Europe. Finally, in 1968, he returned to his native land under the protection of an amnesty. At Pau, one of his junior officers said to him, "Vous n'avez rien à faire ici.... Vous êtes un

---

[51] According to André Passeron in his book *De Gaulle 1958-1969*, the president stated that he had always intended to give Algeria its independence, but that in 1958 when he went to Algiers he could not, for political reasons, have said so—"il a fallu que je prenne des précautions." See Chateau-Jobert, *Feux et Lumière*, p. 233.

salaud, un lâche et un traître."[52] Today, several books and an autobiog-
raphy later, Chateau-Jobert's distrust of politicians remains un-
diminished, his attitude unrepentant, his conviction in the moral
rightness of his action unchanged.

It is not my purpose to argue whether William Douglas Home and
Pierre Chateau-Jobert were right or wrong in what they did. My point
is simply that both men, both of them army officers, were prepared to
follow the dictates of their conscience and to carry their convictions
beyond physical hurt to the extremes of mental suffering and
distress—an even greater test of moral courage than death itself.[53]

----

[52] Ibid., p. 341. This kind of "mésacceuil" proved to be the exception rather than
the rule. Not long after his return to France, Chateau-Jobert was formally retired from
the French army on pension. There were obviously many who sympathized with him.
General Massu had remarked to Chateau-Jobert, "C'est drôle, tout le monde vous
aime..." (p. 342).

[53] Mackenzie, *On Moral Courage*, pp. 12, 153. In 1862 Sir James Fitzjames Stephen
(later Mr. Justice Stephen) wrote in an essay, "Moral courage is readiness to expose
oneself to suffering or inconvenience which does not affect the body. It arises from
firmness of moral principle and is independent of the physical constitution." He was
making the point that mental suffering or opprobrium were harder to bear than physical
hurts. I have not dealt with the question of whether selective conscientious objection
should qualify for exemption from military service. This was decided in the United States
in the case of the *United States v. Gillette*, 401 U.S. 437, 1971. See D. Malament, "Selective
Conscientious Objectors and the *Gillette* decision," in Cohen, Nagel, and Scanlon (eds.),
War and Moral Responsibility, pp. 159-82. The author of the article was imprisoned for
refusing induction into the American army. His article should be read with this fact in
mind. The orders given to the commanders of the British and American armies after
Yalta, for the return—forcible if necessary—of all Russian prisoners, and in particular
the Cossacks and soldiers who had served under Krasnov and Vlasov against the Soviet
forces, were resisted by several senior officers, notably, Maj.-Gen. Horatius Murray of the
6th Br. Armoured Division, Field Marshalls Alexander and Montgomery, and the Supreme Commander, General Eisenhower. See Nicolai Tolstoy, *Victims of Yalta* (London,
1977), pp. 265-66, 273-74, 345. The result was considerable tension between the army
and the Foreign Office. To the generals the issue was a moral one, for the repatriation of
the prisoners meant certain death, as Alexander Solzhenitsyn later pointed out in *The
Gulag Archipelago* (London, 1974).

FOR KING AND COUNTRY: THE LIMITS OF LOYALTY OF BRITISH OFFICERS IN THE WAR FOR AMERICAN INDEPENDENCE

IRA D. GRUBER

HISTORIANS HAVE long recognized that the War for American Independence forced many British officers to make difficult decisions—to decide between their duty as officers and their principles or inclinations as British subjects. Because Anglo-American differences had been debated for more than a decade before fighting began, many officers had by 1775 taken sides in that debate; even the most apolitical had by then considered that they might one day be called upon to serve against the colonists. The prospect of prolonged service overseas in a difficult and relatively primitive country was in itself disagreeable for many officers. But the prospect of bearing arms against other British subjects—and in support of what some said were dubious governmental policies—gave pause even to some of those who had devoted their lives to the army and were eager for preferment.[1]

To illustrate how these prospects affected individual officers, historians have turned repeatedly to a few prominent men. Colonel James Grant is considered typical of those who favoured coercive measures and welcomed an opportunity to serve. Authoritarian by nature and contemptuous of the colonists, Grant told the House of Commons that with 5,000 men he would march from one end of the continent to the other. Jeffery Lord Amherst represents those who supported the ministry's policies but refused to command in America. He was unwilling to risk his marriage and military reputation in what he thought a most unpromising war. Conversely, General William Howe opposed coercion but accepted command. A sense of military obligation and a desire to promote a peaceful settlement seem to have overcome his reluctance to go to America.[2] Others carried their opposition to the use of force considerably further. Lord George Henry Lennox, following the lead of his brother, the Duke of Richmond, denounced the war,

---

[1] As early as February 1766, Lieutenant General George Howard told the House of Commons that he would kill himself before he would command against Englishmen in North America, against "his countrymen who were contending for *English* liberty." Sir Lewis Namier and John Brooke, *The House of Commons, 1754-1790*, 3 vols. (New York, 1964), vol. 2, p. 645.

[2] Namier and Brooke, *House of Commons*, vol. 2, p. 530; J. C. Long, *Lord Jeffery Amherst a Soldier of the King* (New York, 1933), chap. 19; Ira D. Gruber, *The Howe Brothers and the American Revolution* (Chapel Hill, 1974), pp. 56-58.

voted against the ministry, and sacrificed advancement in the army. And Charles Lee, a lieutenant-colonel on half pay who had moved to Virginia in 1773, joined the Continental army and resigned his British commission.[3]

All of this is well known. What is not known—indeed what has never been studied systematically—is how attitudes toward the American rebellion and the ministry's coercive policies affected British officers in general. What were the responsibilities of a commissioned officer? Did loyalty to king and country and the obligation to obey a superior require that officers suppress all private views? If not, what might an officer do when ordered to act against his personal or political beliefs? What *did* officers do during the American War? Were they, for example, able to change regiments to avoid serving against the colonists; or were they forced to choose between serving in America and quitting the service? Did this war produce more instability within the officer corps than wars waged exclusively with other nations? If so, did that instability affect the performance of the army in America? Finally, were senior officers, the men who commanded armies at Boston, New York, or Charleston, inhibited by a sense of duty or loyalty? Did they feel peculiarly bound to follow the direction of king and minister; or were they, by virtue of high rank, freer than their subordinates to question or depart from governmental policies? This essay attempts to answer these questions, to examine the relationship between personal views and public obligations in a revolutionary war, and to see how that relationship affected the performance of an officer corps.

It is, to be sure, far easier to ask than to answer these questions. There were at the outset of the American War approximately 3,500 commissioned officers in the British army. These officers were assigned to four troops and five regiments of cavalry, twenty-one regiments of dragoons, and seventy-three regiments of foot, as well as to assorted units of invalids, artillery, engineers, and marines.[4] It is relatively easy, using the lists printed annually after 1754, to identify these officers; it is more difficult to establish where they were serving. Furthermore, it is frequently impossible to discover their attitudes toward the war and military service. The annual lists provide a complete roster of officers and the location of each unit. But these lists do not make

---

[3]Namier and Brooke, *House of Commons*, vol. 3, pp. 35-36; John Richard Alden, *General Charles Lee: Traitor or Patriot?* (Baton Rouge, [1951]), chaps. 4-5.

[4] *A List of the General and Field-Officers, As They Rank in the Army; of the Officers in the Several Regiments of Horse, Dragoons, and Foot, on the British and Irish Establishments . . . for 1774* (London [1774]). Although titles of lists vary slightly from year to year, the lists from the Seven Years War through the War for American Independence were published invariably by J. Millan, are similar in content, and will be referred to hereafter as *List of the Army* for the appropriate year(s).

clear whether an officer was actually with his unit.[5] Nor do they reflect promptly the transfers of officers from one regiment to another; and only rarely do they explain why an officer changed units or left the army. In short, the lists are indispensable in identifying individual officers and gauging trends within the army, in measuring rates of attrition and reassignment. They must, however, be used with other sources of biographical data in judging the delicate interplay of personal views, duty, and performance in the officer corps as a whole.

Before examining what officers did during the Revolution, it is important to ask what they were required and expected to do, what obligations went with a commission. The commission itself—that is, the document appointing a man to a particular rank—described an officer's duty in very general terms. In appointing Roger Townshend Colonel of Foot in North America in 1758, William Pitt expressed confidence in Townshend's "Loyalty, Courage & Experience in Military Affairs," authorized him to act as a colonel, and bound him to do his "Duty" and to obey his superiors according to "the Rules & Discipline of War."[6] The "Rules & Discipline of War," set forth in small printed books informally called the "Articles of War," were only slightly more specific. The Articles made clear that an officer was to be loyal to his church and king and obedient to his commanding officer: blasphemy and disrespect were punishable by court-martial; mutiny, sedition, disobedience, desertion, cowardice before the enemy, and plundering, by death.[7] But neither the Articles nor custom prevented an officer from taking an active part in politics, holding a seat in Parliament, and voting as he wished. Occasionally an officer was deprived of a military sinecure for opposing the king and the ministry on an important question; only rarely was he stripped of command because of his views.[8] Loyalty to the king did not require than an officer suppress his views on great issues like the American War.

---

[5] A comparison of Worthington Chauncey Ford, *British Officers Serving in the American Revolution* (Brooklyn, 1897), with Namier and Brooke, *House of Commons* reveals the hazards of relying exclusively and uncritically on the annual printed lists. Ford includes in his list of officers serving in America many who remained at home throughout the war, and he excludes some who left their regular units to serve on the staff of the Commander-in-Chief or in one of the several units created exclusively for service in the colonies.

[6] William Pitt to Roger Townshend, August 24, 1758, Townshend Papers 297/6, William L. Clements Library, Ann Arbor, Michigan.

[7] *Rules and Articles for the Better Government of His Majesty's Horse and Foot Guards and all other His Forces in Great Britain and Ireland, and Dominions beyond the Seas For the Year 1745* (London, 1745). An earlier abstract of the "Articles of War," which is very similar to the edition of 1745, is in *The New Art of War* (London, 1726).

[8] In 1756 George II dismissed Sir Henry Erskine from the army for voting against the ministry in the House of Commons; and George Grenville subsequently deprived several officers of sinecures for voting against him: Thomas Calcraft lost his post as

Although a commission and the Articles of War did not require
more than loyalty, courage, experience, and obedience, officers knew
that more was expected of them—that all save aging colonels and
general officers without commands were expected to be with their
regiments or to serve in some other capacity during times of crisis. In
The Cadet, a manual for young officers published in 1756, Major
Samuel Bever said it would be shameful for an officer to refuse to
embark on "any Expedition whatever, especially where the Service of
his King and the Welfare of his Country require it."⁹ Bever was a
reformer, but his views were shared by many prominent officers serving during the American War. In 1774 Colonel Hugh Lord Percy
insisted on accompanying his regiment to Boston even though his
parents opposed his going—his mother asked the king to excuse
him—and even though he, while favouring the continuation of British
rule in America, was highly critical of the ministry's colonial policies.
Percy said simply: "It was his indispensable duty to accompany his
regiment."¹⁰ Major-General William Howe used very similar language
in justifying his decision to serve as second in command at Boston: "I
was ordered and could not refuse, without incurring the odious name
of backwardness to serving my country in day of distress." Howe was
not telling the whole truth—he had, in fact, sought command—but he
was trying to be plausible.¹¹

Whatever was required and expected of them, some officers were
able to avoid disagreeable service; but few among them sought to deny
their responsibility to serve or expected that they could refuse with
impunity. Colonel Staats Long Morris seems to have been an exception.
Because he was a staunch supporter of the ministry and because his
brothers were leading patriots in New York, he was apparently allowed
to remain in England. Some other prominent officers who opposed the
ministry's American policy, but who also felt an obligation to serve,
managed to postpone active duty until France entered the war.
Lieutenant-Colonel Ralph Abercromby was one of them: he stayed in
Ireland until 1778, avoiding, as his son put it, "a conflict between his

---

aide-de camp to the lord lieutenant of Ireland and Henry Seymour Conway, his colo-
nelcy of a regiment and place in the king's bedchamber. But once Grenville fell from
power, officers seemed to suffer less for their political views. For opposing the North
ministry in 1780 George Augustus Herbert was merely delayed in obtaining a commission in the guards. Namier and Brooke, *House of Commons*, vol. 2, pp. 403, 175, 244, 611.

⁹ [Samuel Bever], *The Cadet* (London, 1762), p. 241.

¹⁰ Namier and Brooke, *House of Commons*, vol. 3, p. 269. From a letter from Lord
Suffolk to King George III, February 11, 1774, in *The Correspondence of King George III
from 1760 to December 1783*, ed. Sir John Fortescue, 6 vols. (London: Macmillan and Co.
Ltd., 1928), vol. 3, pp. 63-64.

¹¹ Howe to Samuel Kirk, February 21, 1775, Franklin Papers, Historical Society of
Pennsylvania, Philadelphia; Gruber, *Howe Brothers*, p. 58.

duty as a soldier and his principles as a citizen."[12] The Earl of Pembroke, another critic of the American War, kept his son Captain George Augustus Herbert abroad until 1780, a virtual prisoner on the grand tour. Young Captain Herbert, feeling a responsibility to join his regiment, asked to come home. Pembroke refused until both France and Spain had declared war.[13] Senior officers or officers with powerful families and friends were, it seems, sometimes able to avoid serving in America without sacrificing more than opportunities to distinguish themselves. Some were even promoted while sitting out the war. Junior officers lacking the right connections were less fortunate: if they were unwilling to serve, they might arrange either to transfer to less desirable regiments or to sell their commissions and retire.[14]

If officers knew what was required and expected of them, and if only senior or well-connected officers could evade disagreeable service with relative impunity, how did British officers in general respond to the American War—to the conflicts that arose between their military obligation and their private views? To evaluate the response of 3,500 men, many of whom were relatively obscure, it has been necessary to pursue several lines of investigation. First, to judge the stability of the officer corps as a whole during the Revolution—to find out whether the army suffered from exceptionally high rates of reassignment and resignation—it seemed desirable to establish those rates for other, similar periods of peace and war. To simplify the task, groups of 100 officers were selected at random from all officers of foot and from all senior officers in the army in 1755, 1766, and 1774. Infantry and senior officers were chosen because they were the officers who served in America; 1755, 1766, and 1774, because they marked the beginnings of comparable periods of war and peace. Each of these groups was then analyzed over time to measure the relative stability of the officer corps before and during the Revolution. Finally, to assess the influence of political and personal views on the behaviour of officers,

---

[12] Namier and Brooke, *House of Commons*, vol. 3, pp. 168-69, and vol. 2, p. 3 (quoting Abercromby's son).

[13] Ibid., vol. 2, pp. 610-11.

[14] Even officers with powerful grievances were forced to acknowledge their obligation to serve the king. In November 1779, after having lost an army and joined the opposition to the North ministry, John Burgoyne complained "that the prevalence of the term the *King's army* and the *King's fleet* in preference to their being called the forces of the state, was one among the many manifestations of the Tory doctrine of this reign." Ibid., vol. 2, p. 145. Indeed, British officers in the era of the American Revolution seem to have had a far greater sense of responsibility to serve than has sometimes been allowed, certainly more than Samuel P. Huntington conceded in *The Soldier and the State* (Cambridge, 1957), chap. 2. Officers clearly felt an obligation to their king and country. They may also have felt an obligation to other officers within their regiment (see James W. Hayes, "The Social and Professional Background of the Officers of the British Army, 1714-1763" [unpublished M.A. thesis, University of London, 1956]).

all officers who were members of Parliament from the Seven Years War to the close of the American Revolution were studied intensively. These officer-members were chosen because they, unlike other officers, were called upon publicly to express their views on the rebellion and the ministry's coercive policies.

Consider first the behaviour of infantry officers in peacetime—specifically, of 100 chosen at random from the 2,240 officers of foot on active service in 1766. An analysis of their regimental assignments, promotions, duty stations, and resignations between 1766 and 1769 reveals a pattern of considerable stability. On average nearly 87 per cent of the officers considered remained·in the same regiment and at the same location from one year to the next. Promotion came slowly—usually to about 6 per cent of the officers in any one year—and most promotions were to vacancies within the same regiment. No more than 12 per cent per year found their peacetime routine disturbed with orders to accompany their regiments to some new post or with promotion to another regiment. If reluctance to leave familiar places—to go from America to Ireland, Ireland to Gibraltar, or England to America—led some to resign, fewer than 6 per cent per year did leave the service. Indeed, British infantry officers led very static lives in the peaceful years between the repeal of the Stamp Act and the Boston Massacre.[15]

What a difference war made in those lives. To judge from the experiences of another group of 100 infantry officers, drawn at random from the 1,754 serving in 1755, the Seven Years War greatly accelerated the pace of promotion and brought new assignments to most officers and many regiments. But the Seven Years War, fought against a traditional enemy in both America and Europe, did not significantly increase resignations. At the beginning of the war, while the government was trying to protect its American colonies without drawing heavily upon forces at home, officers enjoyed rapid promotion (25 per cent were promoted in 1756 alone) and, with few exceptions, the continuation of peacetime assignments. Nearly 80 per cent remained in the same regiment and at the same post throughout 1756 and 1757; and only about 13 per cent per year were required to move. But once the ministry decided to create new regiments, double the forces in North America, and begin sending troops to Germany, officers were reassigned at a bewildering rate. In 1758 only 31 per cent escaped dislocation: 40 per cent were sent with their regiments to new posts, and another 19 per cent changed regiments. What did remain

---

[15] One hundred officers of foot were chosen at random from *A List of the Army for 1766* and pursued through the lists for 1767, 1768, and 1769. Summary tables of the data gathered for this essay are on file at the Woodson Research Center, Fondren Library, Rice University.

remarkably constant even during the rapid mobilization of 1758 was the rate of officer resignation. That rate (about 8 per cent in 1758) was only slightly higher than it had been in 1756 and 1757 (when it was between 7 and 8 per cent) or would be in the late 1760s (6 per cent per year); and few among those resigning in 1756, 1757, or 1758 did so to avoid overseas service.[16]

While British infantry officers seem to have responded very positively to the demands and opportunities of the Seven Years War, their response to the War for American Independence would be quite different. To generalize once again from the experiences of 100 officers of foot (chosen in this instance from the 2,345 serving in 1774), British officers were much less willing to serve in 1776 than they had been in 1758. At the beginning of the American War, while the North ministry sought to intimidate Massachusetts with troops drawn mainly from garrisons in the colonies, few demands were made on the army as a whole. Eighty-seven per cent of infantry officers were serving in 1775 where they had been the year before: reassignments and promotions were well below the averages for the opening years of the Seven Years War. But even in 1775, when little was asked of most officers, resignations were higher (at 9 per cent) than they had been between 1755 and 1758; and they would go higher still in 1776 when the ministry made a determined effort to crush the rebellion. In addition to hiring thousands of German troops for the campaign of 1776, the ministry increased its own forces in the colonies from thirteen to thirty-four regiments. Such a rapid concentration of so large a portion of the entire British army (there were only seventy regiments in 1776) required sweeping reassignments of officers and men. Nearly 40 per cent of all officers were ordered to accompany their regiments to some new post, usually in North America. Forced to decide whether they would command against other British subjects in a remote and difficult country, many resigned. The rate of resignation rose in 1776 to more than 16 per cent or twice the rate for 1758; and of the 16 per cent, more than three fourths were officers whose regiments had been ordered to America or who had been serving in America when fighting began at Lexington.[17]

What were the consequences of these resignations? In retrospect it would seem that so many resignations in so short a time would have damaged the morale and disrupted the internal order of many regiments and, perhaps, affected the performance of the whole army in the campaigns of 1776 and 1777. Surely when five of thirty officers in a

---

[16] These conclusions are drawn from an analysis of the service of 100 officers of foot taken at random from *A List of the Army for 1755* and observed through the lists for 1756, 1757, and 1758.

[17] *A List of the Army for 1774* and lists for 1775, 1776, and 1777.

regiment resign within a matter of months, and when most do so out of distaste for the service ahead, the whole regiment must suffer. Old officers must assume new duties; new officers must be worked in; and officers and men alike must reexamine their attitudes toward the war as well as their obligations to the king and their regiment. Moreover, all of this had to be done under the most difficult circumstances. Most resignations seem to have come just when regiments in the British Isles were preparing to embark for America or, in several cases, when regiments already at Boston or Halifax were preparing for the campaign of 1776 at New York.[18]

Although morale and internal order probably did suffer in some regiments, the effects of the resignations of 1776 were not as severe or long lasting as they might have been. Consider first morale. Most of those who resigned in 1776 were junior officers, usually lieutenants but also some ensigns. With perhaps no more than six or seven years invested in an army career, these, among all officers, had the least to lose by deciding not to serve; conversely, they, among all, had the least prospect of being able to avoid serving in America without quitting the army. Their resignations may well have affected the morale of ordinary soldiers: although there was considerable distance between officers and men in the army of George III, the men were thought capable of thinking and feeling.[19] But the resignations of many junior officers may also have improved the morale of officers collectively and, by extension, of the army as a whole. Removing those junior officers who were most reluctant to serve left the regiments in the hands of officers with a greater commitment to the service and, perhaps, to the American War. It also created vacancies to be filled with newly commissioned officers, with young gentlemen who would have had ample time *before* buying commissions to decide whether they wished to sustain royal government in America. No wonder then that the principal area of complaint of officers in late 1776 and in 1777 would be with the lack of progress in the war rather than with the war itself.[20]

Resignations did not seriously damage morale, but they probably would have disrupted the internal order of many regiments had not the king fortuitously intervened. Regiments usually lost, through resignations, about two officers per year in peacetime and, through a combination of resignations and transfers, as many as five or six per

---

[18] Ibid.

[19] John Burgoyne based his training on the assumption that English soldiers were rational beings who would respond positively to the notice of their officers. Edward Barrington de Fonblanque, *Political and Military Episodes . . . from the Life and Correspondence of . . . John Burgoyne, General, Statesman, Dramatist* (London, 1876), pp. 15-22.

[20] Gruber, *Howe Brothers*, pp. 124, 133, 147, 206-207, 224-26, 229-30, 236, 254-56. Nor should it be astonishing that very few British officers deserted during the Revolution: morale was simply too high among those who went to America to nourish thoughts

year during a war. Quite by chance, the flood of resignations in 1776 was not accompanied by the usual wartime increase in inter-regimental transfers. Because George III had refused to create new regiments in 1775—preferring instead to provide troops for the American War by enlarging existing regiments and hiring foreigners—no officers were transferred from old to new regiments in 1776; and transfers between existing regiments did not exceed 1 per cent. Had the king followed the example of his grandfather and authorized new regiments, the combination of resignations and transfers together might have taken more than one third of the officers from many regiments. As it was, the total drain on most regiments (about five officers in 1776) was below the average for the opening years of the Seven Years War (six per year) and well below that for 1758, when transfers and resignations took an average eight officers from each regiment of foot. In addition, the high tide of resignations of 1776 receded as quickly as it had risen. Even though another nine regiments embarked for America in late 1776 and in 1777, and even though nearly 30 per cent of all infantry officers were once again reassigned with their regiments, resignations dropped to 9 per cent in 1777—to the level of 1775 and not far above that for 1758.[21]

This analysis of infantry officers in general might suggest that senior officers responded somewhat differently to the Revolution than did their juniors—at least, that majors, lieutenant-colonels, and colonels were not among those quitting the army in 1776. But is this suggestion sound? How, specifically, did general and field officers respond to the Revolution? It is, of course, more difficult to measure the response of senior officers because many of them—perhaps 40 per cent—did not see active service during the Revolution and because those who did were frequently able to avoid disagreeable assignments without resigning from the army.[22] Nevertheless, a comparison of the

---

of desertion; and those who served elsewhere rarely had the incentive or the opportunity to join the rebels. It is true that a number of prominent officers in continental service had once held regular commissions in the British army—Horatio Gates, Edward Hand, Moses Hazen, Richard Humpton, Charles Lee, Richard Montgomery, and Arthur St. Clair among them. But only Charles Lee and an obscure assistant engineer named Thomas Hutchins are known to have changed sides after fighting began, to have resigned their British commissions after Lexington. Mark Mayo Boatner, *Encyclopedia of the American Revolution* (New York [1966]), pp. 412-16, 484-85, 497-98, 534, 605-607, 726-27, 956-57. On Thomas Hutchins see Douglas William Marshall, "The British Military Engineers 1741-1783: A Study of Organization, Social Origin, and Cartography" (unpublished Ph.D. dissertation, University of Michigan, 1976), p. 293.

[21] For the king's decision see Gruber, *Howe Brothers*, p. 29. The comparative data on resignations and transfers is drawn from the random samples of 100 officers of foot from the lists for 1755-1758, 1766-1769, and 1774-1777.

[22] Random sample of 100 general and field officers from *A List of the Army for 1774* pursued through the lists for 1775, 1776, and 1777.

reactions of senior officers to the Seven Years War and to the War for American Independence suggests that they, like officers of foot, served more willingly in 1758 than in 1776. In 1758, to judge from a sample of 100 of the 377 general and field officers in the list of 1755, senior officers did what little was asked of them. At a time when nearly 70 per cent of all infantry officers were being ordered to new posts or regiments, only 9 per cent of majors, colonels, and generals were undertaking new commands or embarking with their regiments; almost all other senior officers remained in the British Isles—in various commands or simply not on active duty. And only one senior officer seems to have left the army to avoid going overseas with his regiment.[23]

In 1776, to judge once more from a random sample (from the actions of 100 of the 624 general and field officers in the army list of 1774), senior officers were not as willing to serve as they had been during the Seven Years War. At least, the rate of resignation among senior officers, which had been 1 per cent per year between 1755 and 1758, now rose to nearly 7 per cent per year; and five of 100 senior officers either resigned from the army or gave up their regimental commands for half pay in order to avoid serving in America. In 1776, when 22 per cent of general and field officers were ordered to new commands or new posts, nearly 10 per cent resigned. These resignations were not often in response to specific orders; and they certainly were not so numerous or threatening as those submitted by junior officers of foot—not at least when only 16 per cent of senior officers were required in America. Morale and authority would survive. But these resignations did represent an unusually large exodus of majors and lieutenant-colonels, of men who it seems lacked the influence to gain further promotion or choice assignments and found retirement preferable to the prospect of service in a difficult war.[24]

Although some officers resigned because they preferred retirement to service in a disagreeable war, many more continued to serve in that war. Did they do so because they believed Britain had a right to govern her American colonies? Or, if they doubted that right or were critical of the ministry's coercive policies, did they serve out of a sense of an officer's obligation to his king and country? Or, is it possible that some were dubious about the war but unwilling to resign and unable to avoid going to the colonies? To answer these questions—at least, to suggest answers—it is necessary to go beyond the army lists to biographies of individual officers—specifically, to biographies of those officers who were also Members of Parliament. There are, it is true,

---

[23] Random sample of 100 general and field officers from *A List of the Army for 1755* followed through the lists for 1756, 1757, and 1758.

[24] This analysis is drawn from a comparison of random samples of 100 general and field officers from the lists for 1755-1758 and 1774-1777.

disadvantages in studying officer-members. They, among all officers, were the most privileged. Many belonged to elite regiments that would be kept at home even in wartime, and most had the kind of influence required to escape unpleasant assignments without sacrificing their careers in the army. Moreover, many were attached to the king—through his household and through lucrative military appointments—and nearly all, as Members of Parliament, had a personal interest in sustaining the power and prestige of that body. Yet it is important to study those officer-members because they provided the indispensable bond between the army and the king in Parliament; and they were the only officers asked not merely to decide whether they would serve in the American War but also to say publicly what they thought of the war.

What, then, did they—the 176 officers who sat in the House of Commons during the American Revolution—think of the colonists' rebellion, the ministry's coercive measures, and their own role in the ensuing conflict?[25] As might be expected of men of wealth, standing, and independence, they held a variety of views on the American rebellion. But they also had a remarkably consistent view of the British empire and of their obligations as officers of the king. A clear majority believed that Britain had a right to govern America, that the king in Parliament was the supreme authority throughout the empire. Of those whose votes are known, nearly 90 per cent opposed the repeal of the Stamp Act in 1766, voting against a conciliatory measure approved by the whole House of Commons, 275 to 167.[26] Although there was much less agreement on how best to secure the dependence of the

---

[25] To be precise, the 176 officers considered were men who held regular commissions (not on half pay) between 1774 and 1783 and who were also Members of Parliament at some time during their lives. Most were Members during the American War; but some, like Charles Cornwallis, who had gone to the House of Lords in 1762, completed their service in the Commons before 1774; and others did not enter the House of Commons until after 1783. Brief political sketches of these 176 officers—sketches from which most of the ensuing generalizations have been drawn—are in Namier and Brooke, *House of Commons*, vol. 2, pp. 3-5, 13, 17, 20, 22, 26, 34, 43, 67, 69, 88-89, 103-105, 141-45, 159, 165, 175, 179-80, 188-90, 197, 198, 200-201, 222-23, 228-29, 239, 244-47, 252, 256-57, 268-69, 283-85, 295-97, 329, 331, 350, 357, 366-67, 384-86, 405-406, 408, 413-14, 416-17, 424, 433, 435-37, 467, 470-72, 481-82, 509-12, 516, 518-19, 523-25, 529-31, 547-48, 551, 553-55, 578, 581, 594-95, 601, 610-12, 620, 628, 635-36, 641-43, 645-46, 649-50, 667, 685-86, 692; vol. 3, 11-12, 18-19, 23-24, 34-36, 63, 65-66, 78, 83-89, 98-99, 107-109, 117-18, 120-21, 137, 148, 149, 151, 157-61, 163-64, 168-69, 176-78, 180-84, 186-87, 189-91, 202-203, 213, 235-36, 249, 257, 261, 263-64, 269, 271-72, 276, 278-79, 281, 302, 326, 346, 363, 368, 374-75, 377-78, 384, 399, 401-402, 405, 413-14, 419, 424, 425, 441-42, 457, 462-63, 467, 473, 477-80, 498-502, 548-52, 576-77, 582-83, 592, 594, 610, 622-23, 646-47, 657, 658, 665-66, 679-80.

[26] For those who voted against repeal see ibid., vol. 2, pp. 88, 125, 142, 189, 329, 364, 471, 511, 524, 594, and vol. 3, pp. 84, 104, 107, 121, 148, 155, 158, 164, 177, 269, 332, 419, 426, 592; those who voted for are in ibid., vol. 2, pp. 51-52, 501, 620.

colonies, nearly 50 per cent of officer-members supported and only 12 per cent opposed the North ministry's coercive policies (the views of the remaining 38 per cent are not known). And once fighting began, nearly all acknowledged and most accepted their obligation to military service. If fewer members went abroad with their regiments and if resignations were slightly higher than in the Seven Years War, more than 20 per cent did serve in America; another 10 per cent in the West Indies and India; and yet another 30 per cent in the British Isles. Altogether, nearly 60 per cent saw active duty and only 12 per cent resigned between 1774 and 1783—an annual rate of resignation (about 1½ per cent per year) that was below the peacetime rate for officer-members.[27]

It must, of course, be asked whether officers' attitudes toward the rebellion and coercive measures controlled what they chose to do as officers. Were those in favour of coercion more likely to serve than those who preferred conciliation? Or, did a uniform sense of military obligation override all political considerations? Consider first those eighty-seven officers who supported the ministry's policies.[28] It is not astonishing that 21 per cent of their number went to America and that another 43 per cent served elsewhere. These officers were, as Major John Dyke Acland said, "convinced of the justice of the British cause" and prepared to use "vigorous measures" to make the colonists submit to royal government.[29] Such officers not only commanded in America, the West Indies, and India but also raised and trained troops at home, especially after France and Spain entered the war. Not all who favoured vigorous measures put duty before personal preference: a few refused to accept command in America, 11 per cent resigned, and 9 per cent did not serve at all. But only two clearly used resignation or half pay to avoid the American War.[30]

What of those who opposed or came to oppose coercion? Several, including Lieutenant-Colonel Ralph Abercromby and Captain George

---

[27] These estimates are based on the performances of the 176 officer-members identified in note 25; the peacetime rate for officer-members has been calculated by studying the 178 officers serving between 1763 and 1773 who are included in Namier and Brooke, *House of Commons*, vol. 2, vol. 3, passim.

[28] The eighty-seven officers (of 176 under consideration) who are known to have supported the ministry's policies are described in Namier and Brooke, *House of Commons*, vol. 2, pp. 4-5, 13, 43, 88-89, 103-104, 141-45, 159, 165, 188-90, 197, 222-23, 228-29, 252, 283-85, 295-97, 329, 366-67, 384-86, 405, 408, 416-17, 435, 437, 470-72, 510-12, 516, 518-19, 529-31, 547, 551, 578, 581, 594-95, 641-43, 645-46, 649-50, 667, 692; vol. 3, 18-19, 23-24, 65-66, 83-89, 98-99, 107-108, 148-49, 160-61, 168-69, 180-81, 184, 189-91, 202-203, 235-36, 249, 257, 261, 263-64, 276, 346, 363, 368, 384, 399, 413-14, 419, 425, 442, 467, 473, 498-502, 548-52, 576-77, 592, 610, 646-47, 679-80.

[29] Ibid., vol. 2, p. 4.

[30] Only James Cunninghame and John Pennington, among those eighty-seven officers supporting the ministry, left regiments that were ordered to America. Ibid., vol. 2, p. 283; vol. 3, pp. 263-64.

Augustus Herbert, managed to avoid active service until France entered the war.[31] But most—indeed, proportionately more than of those supporting coercion—served from the beginning: 18 per cent in America, 41 per cent at home, and 14 per cent in other parts of the empire—a total of 73 per cent of those twenty-two officers who opposed the war.[32] That proportionately more critics than proponents should have served and that proportionately fewer sought to escape serving demonstrates both the importance attached to duty and the cost of opposition to the ministry. An officer who spoke or voted against the war in Parliament could not expect any concessions from the king or the ministry. If his regiment were ordered abroad, he would be forced either to serve or to resign; and resigning—refusing to accept his responsibilities as an officer—seems to have been unacceptable to a man who thought of himself as a responsible critic of coercive policies. Thus Captain Richard Fitzpatrick, who described North's policies as "ruinous," went with his regiment to the colonies in 1777, distinguished himself, and then returned home to renew his attacks on the ministry and the war.[33] Similarly, those who remained at home and came to oppose the ministry during the war, were eager to serve—to show by raising a regiment or volunteering for duty that they were responsible officers and that their criticism of the American War was more than factious ranting.[34] Those who became opponents of the war while serving in America—men like Colonel John Wrottesley—did not have to prove they were responsible; they could concentrate on proposing alternatives to conquest.[35]

A sense of duty seems to have been enough to impel many a reluctant officer to the colonies. But was it enough to ensure that he would not allow his reservations about the war to influence his performance in it? It is, of course, impossible to know how most officers sought to reconcile differences between their private views and their public responsibilities. It is possible to ask how the few who had independent commands met their responsibilities, their obligation to obey the king and carry out the ministry's coercive policies.

Those who commanded at the beginning of the war, before fighting had confirmed differences between mother country and colonies, seem to have had the greatest difficulty keeping their private sympathy for the colonists and their hopes for reconciliation from affecting their public actions. General Thomas Gage, commanding at Boston in 1775,

---

[31] Ibid., vol. 2, pp. 3-4, 610-12.

[32] Sketches of the twenty-two are in ibid., vol. 2, pp. 3-5, 22, 244-47, 256, 357, 433, 548, 553-55, 601, 610-12, 635-36, and vol. 3, pp. 11, 35-36, 63, 137, 269, 271-72, 377-78, 463, 473, 665-66.

[33] Ibid., vol. 2, p. 433.

[34] Ibid., vol. 2, p. 357; vol. 3, pp. 377-78, 473.

[35] Ibid., vol. 3, pp. 665-66.

was a staunch advocate of parliamentary supremacy as well as a firm friend of many colonists. Believing that the colonists should bear some of the costs of imperial defence, he had favoured the Stamp Act and Townshend duties, urged using force to crush opposition to taxation, and volunteered in 1774 to carry out coercive measures. But in nearly twenty years of continuous service in America, he had also married into a New Jersey family, bought land in New York, Nova Scotia, and the West Indies, and made many friends. It is understandable, therefore, that he should have continued to discuss concessions while he prepared for and started a war. It is also understandable that the ministry should have thought him too moderate and removed him from command soon after the battle of Bunker Hill.[36] General Guy Carleton, who commanded in Canada at the beginning of the war, was even more moderate than Gage. Carleton certainly wished to sustain British authority in America and he exerted himself fully in defending Canada and in helping Burgoyne prepare for the campaign of 1777. Yet he thought persuasion as important as force in retaining America. During the winter of 1775 he refused to loose Indians on the frontiers of New England even though they might have helped him save Quebec; and the following summer, he restrained his own forces from pressing the rebels retreating from Canada. These conciliatory gestures impressed neither the colonists nor the ministry. He too was recalled.[37]

The ministry could remove Gage and Carleton for being too moderate, but it could scarcely charge either of them with failing to do his duty. Both had tried to sustain royal government with inadequate forces and without full or clear instructions. Neither had deliberately departed from the ministry's plans. Such would not be the case with General William Howe, Gage's successor. Howe, more than any British commander during the Revolution, allowed his—or at least his family's—affection for the colonists and his preference for conciliation to interfere with clearly stated plans of campaign. It is possible that Howe, who led the attack at Bunker Hill and who had intimate knowledge of colonial resentment, would *not* have deviated from his instructions without pressure from his family. During the winter of 1775-1776 he and Lord George Germain had agreed completely on a plan for 1776. Howe would go to New York not merely to take the city, push up the Hudson, and isolate the rebellion in New England, but primarily to precipitate a decisive battle "than which [he said], nothing is more to be desired or sought for by us, as the most effectual means to terminate this expensive War. . . ." But before Howe could carry out his plan, he

---

[36] John Richard Alden, *General Gage in America* . . . (Baton Rouge, 1948), chaps. 3, 5, 7, 9-17.

[37] A. G. Bradley, *Lord Dorchester* (New York, 1926), chaps. 4-9 (esp. pp. 146, 203); Boatner, *Encyclopedia of the American Revolution*, p. 560.

was joined at New York by his brother, Admiral Richard Lord Howe. The Admiral, ignorant of the rebellion and filled with enthusiasm for conciliation, soon sapped the general's preference for a decisive battle. At least, after Lord Howe arrived, General Howe repeatedly spurned opportunities to destroy the Continental army—at Long Island, on Manhattan, and in New Jersey—and talked no more of a climactic battle until the campaign and conciliatory efforts had ended disastrously at Trenton and Princeton. In 1777 Howe again chose to depart from what he knew to be the ministry's plan and was recalled.[38]

All who rose to command after Howe had once shared his preference for a negotiated settlement. But by the time they came to have independent commands, they had served in at least two campaigns and were not seriously tempted by illusions of reconciliation. Thus Burgoyne, Clinton, and Cornwallis were able—to a remarkable degree—to keep their attitudes toward the rebellion and sympathy for the colonists from interfering with their conduct of the war. It is true that Burgoyne's interest in negotiation was superficial. Having supported the Stamp Act, Declaratory Act, and coercive measures, he offered to act as a roving commissioner of peace only after finding that he would have to serve under Gage or Howe or Clinton. Once he got his own command in Canada, he said no more of negotiations, planned an entirely conventional campaign, and insisted on following the orders he had written to the destruction of his army.[39] Although Clinton seems to have had a deeper interest in conciliation, he decided while serving as second to Howe that destruction of the Continental army would have to precede any meaningful negotiation. As Commander-in-Chief he did resist advice from the ministry and refused to shift the centre of the war to the South—but not because he attached more importance to conciliation than they. Rather, being skeptical of relying on the Loyalists to help win the war, he kept his army together on the Hudson (more than 70 per cent of all the troops in the thirteen colonies remained at New York until late 1780) and ever dreamed of a decisive battle with Washington.[40] Cornwallis certainly did not agree with Clinton's strategy; however, he too put aside his private views while commanding against the rebels. One of only five peers to oppose the Declaratory Act, he volunteered for the American War and commanded with more

---

[38] Gruber, *Howe Brothers*, chaps. 2-9 (quoting p. 83).

[39] Fonblanque, *Political and Military Episodes*, chaps. 4-7; George Athan Billias, "John Burgoyne: Ambitious General," in George Athan Billias (ed.), *George Washington's Opponents: British Generals and Admirals of the American Revolution* (New York, 1969), chap. 5; Namier and Brooke, *House of Commons*, vol. 2, 141-45.

[40] William B. Willcox, *Portrait of a General, Sir Henry Clinton in the War of Independence* (New York, 1964), chaps. 1, 3, 7-10; Ira D. Gruber, "Britain's Southern Strategy," in W. Robert Higgins (ed.), *The Revolutionary War in the South: Power, Conflict, and Leadership* (Durham, 1979), pp. 220-38.

vigour than any other British general. He may have been too humane for partisan warfare. He did crush Gates's army at Camden and he did pursue Greene relentlessly across the Carolina countryside. He failed at last but he adhered consistently to the plans of the ministry—if not always to those of his Commander-in-Chief.[41]

Few British officers genuinely welcomed the American War. Some resigned rather than serve, and a few arranged to serve elsewhere or to avoid active duty until France entered the war. But most did serve; and the morale and internal order of regiments survived surprisingly well. They did so in part because most who left the service were quite junior and were replaced by men willing to go to America; in part because resignations did not coincide with the creation of new regiments; and in part because many prominent officers—officers who were also Members of Parliament—seem to have felt a strong sense of obligation to serve. These officers and others connected with them through family or friendship ensured that the army would be loyal, would do its duty to king and country. But if duty took officers and men to America, it did not keep some of the most important officers from pursuing their private hopes for peace to the detriment of the ministry's plans for destroying the rebellion. Even so, Howe alone among British commanders worked directly against the instructions he received in order to limit fighting and encourage a negotiated peace.

---

[41] Franklin and Mary Wickwire, *Cornwallis: The American Adventure* (Boston, 1970), chaps. 3, 6-16; Namier and Brooke, *House of Commons*, vol. 2, p. 256.

THE ROYAL OFFICER CORPS AND THE FRENCH REVOLUTION

SAMUEL F. SCOTT

LIKE OTHER institutions of the French state in the late eighteenth century, the Royal Army reflected the structure of Old Regime society. The most striking example of this was the complete dominance exercised by the nobility over the officer corps. Not only did nobles provide the vast majority of all officers, but the spirit that permeated this group was also singularly aristocratic. Service as an officer was traditionally regarded as the birthright of the ancient warrior caste.

The army had long afforded one of the few socially acceptable occupations for French nobles; and in the later eighteenth century, as customary sources of income fell behind rising prices, military service became more and more an economic necessity for many aristocrats. Yet, for the nobility of the Old Regime the army did not constitute a career in the modern sense of the term. Their concept of an officer considered serving in the army a primary, but not exclusive, function. Military service was frequently interrupted by extensive leaves; each officer was entitled to seven and a half months' absence every other year and could expect additional leaves if his situation (e.g., family affairs, illness, other public service) required them. Even when on active duty, noble officers had private lodgings and normally spent more time in the society of their civilian peers than with the soldiers whom they commanded.[1]

The only significant non-noble element in the officer corps came from the *officiers de fortune*, who constituted about 10 per cent of its personnel and always occupied a peculiar position within this body.[2] These officers, promoted from the ranks after long and able service, had the closest contact with the troops since they bore most responsibility for recruitment, drill, discipline, and supply in their regiments. They rarely rose above the grade of lieutenant and in 1788 legislation formally prohibited them from becoming captains. Another ordinance

---

[1] Raoul Griardet, *La Société militaire dans la France contemporaine (1815-1939)* (Paris, 1953), p. 54; and Serge-William Serman and Jean-Paul Bertaud, *Vie et psychologie des combattants et gens de guerre* (Paris, 1970), p. 58.

[2] The best treatment of this subject is Charles J. Wrong, "The *Officiers de Fortune* in the French Infantry," *French Historical Studies*, vol. 9 (Spring 1976), pp. 400-31. As Wrong notes, a small percentage of these officers were themselves noble.

of the same year excluded regimental colour-bearers and quarter-masters (drawn exclusively from the officers of fortune) from taking the regular leave that all other officers received in alternate years.[3] Furthermore, it is highly unlikely that their fellow officers ever considered the ex-rankers their equals in any respect. In both their functions and treatment the officers of fortune resembled the non-commissioned officers (N.C.O.s), from whose ranks they had been drawn, more than they did the nobles directly commissioned into the army.

The blatant distinctions between the dominant noble majority and subordinate commoner minority were not, however, the only important differences among officers of the Royal Army. Indeed, for most officers a much more pertinent distinction was the privilege enjoyed by nobles who had been presented at court. These aristocrats alone could expect to become colonels or general officers. The provincial nobles, who provided most regimental officers, had to restrict their aspirations to attaining a lieutenant-colonelcy at best; and most would end their careers as captains.[4] A separate but related problem for the lower nobility was the financial expenditure necessary for a successful career. Officers sometimes needed an independent income to maintain themselves as befitted their station, and certainly required money to purchase venal positions, if they hoped for anything beyond very slow and limited advancement.[5] Court influence and wealth thus created a strong sense of frustration on the part of numerous officers and contributed to their growing demand for military reform in the second half of the eighteenth century.

The proponents of reform—largely but not solely provincial nobles—advocated a more competent and dedicated officer corps.[6] In order to achieve this, they wanted the expansion of military schools and the selection of officers from families where military service was a long-established tradition. Once commissioned, officers would thereafter be promoted on the basis of their performance. Thus, ability and devotion would replace wealth and influence. While such attitudes were, in a way, quite professional, the ancient prejudice that identified nobles and officers was maintained. Although the reformers would allow some commoners to become officers of fortune as in the past,

[3] Archives de la Guerre (henceforth, A.G.), *Ordonnances militaires*, vol. 64, royal decision of September 12, 1788.

[4] Arthur Chuquet, "Roture et noblesse dans l'armée royale," *Séances et travaux de l'Académie des sciences morales et politiques*, vol. 175 (1911), p. 237; and Louis Tuetey, *Les Officiers sous l'ancien régime* (Paris, 1908), pp. 33-34.

[5] André Corvisier, "Hiérarchie militaire et hiérarchie sociale à la veille de la Révolution," *Revue Internationale d'Histoire Militaire*, no. 30 (1970), pp. 79-80.

[6] David D. Bien, "La Réaction aristocratique avant 1789: l'exemple de l'armée," *Annales, Economies, Sociétés, Civilisations*, vol. 29 (1974), pp. 23-48, 505-34.

they wanted the officer corps as a whole to retain its basically aristocratic composition.

As the pressure for reform mounted within the army, it was intensified by the stunning defeat suffered by France in the Seven Years War. As a result, the twenty-five years that preceded the outbreak of the Revolution witnessed extensive changes in the French army, although these did not necessarily conform to the nobles' desires. The central government increased its control over the military by assuming direct responsibility for the recruitment and maintenance of troops, by establishing its right to appoint all majors and lieutenant-colonels on an army-wide (rather than on a regimental) basis, and by providing for the gradual elimination of venality. The monarchy also improved military efficiency by reducing the strength of expensive household units and the excessive number of officer positions in the line army. During the same period, royal legislation required four generations of nobility for direct appointment as an officer—excepting officers of fortune—and maintained the court aristocracy's monopoly of the ranks of colonel and general.[7]

Despite the organizational improvements that resulted from these reforms, almost all elements of the officer corps found grounds for objecting to them. The court aristocracy resented the reductions in the prestigious, but largely ceremonial, royal household troops. Provincial nobles continued to chafe at the privileges accorded the nobles presented at court. Commoners saw their hopes of social advancement by way of an army career further limited. All officers were frustrated by the decrease in officer positions, which restricted opportunities for promotion.[8]

By the late 1780s there existed among army officers a marked, but complicated, sense of hostility toward the monarchy. When the noble-dominated high courts of France, the *parlements*, openly defied the King in 1788, a number of officers gave evidence of their sympathy for the noble judges. At Grenoble, Toulouse, Pau, and Besançon officers refused to deploy their troops against anti-government demonstrators; and at Rennes some officers resigned their commissions rather than repress similar disturbances in support of the local *parlement*.[9] Thus,

---

[7] Emile G. Léonard, *L'Armée et ses problèmes au XVIIIᵉ siècle* (Paris, 1958), pp. 239-41; P. Clalmin, "La Désintégration de l'armée royale en France à la fin du XVIIIᵉ siècle," *Revue historique de l'armée* (February 1964), pp. 76-77; François Sicard, *Histoire des institutions militaires des Français*, vol. 2 (Paris, 1834), p. 75; Henri Choppin, *Les Insurrections militaires en 1790* (Paris, 1903), pp. 34-35; and Tuetey, *Officiers*, p. 192.

[8] Albert Latreille, *L'Armée et la nation à la fin de l'ancien régime* (Paris, 1914), p. 77; Henry-Joseph de Buttet, "Le Comité de la brigade de cavalerie en garnison à Strasbourg (août 1789)," *Actes du quatre-vingt-douzième congrès national des sociétés savantes: Strasbourg et Colmar, 1967* (Paris, 1970), p. 386; and Tuetey, *Officiers*, pp. 180-81.

[9] Chalmin, "Désintégration de l'armée," p. 81; Jacques Godechot, *La Grande Nation: L'Expansion révolutionnaire de la France dans le monde, 1789–1799*, vol. 1 (Paris,

officers gave the example of insubordination, an example their men
would not be slow to follow in the crucial times ahead. More immediately, because the regular army was the only police agency in the
country capable of dealing with widespread or large-scale disorders,
the officers' actions undermined the authority of the King.

Faced by a financial crisis bordering on bankruptcy, growing opposition to his policies, and the disturbing attitude of a number of army
officers, Louis XVI in August 1788 agreed to summon, for the first
time in 175 years, a meeting of the Estates General. This decision gave
rise to unprecedented political activity in 1788 and 1789 and encouraged a flood of diverse, and sometimes contradictory, expectations.
The most extraordinary development in this period was the emergence
of the Third Estate as a self-conscious political force. The vast non-
noble, non-clerical majority of the nation for the first time asserted its
right to play an active role in politics, which for centuries had been
dominated by the struggle between monarchy and aristocracy. The
threat thus posed to the established political and social system, that
sustained and justified their special status, rallied most nobles—albeit
belatedly—to the cause of the monarchy.

From the first sessions of the Estates General in the beginning of
May until the last week of June 1789, a deadlock developed between
the King, now supported by most of his nobility, and the Third Estate,
which was gaining the support of most of the clerical deputies of the
First Estate. In late June Louis XVI decided to break the deadlock by
force; within a week he ordered more than 16,000 line troops to the
Paris area to join 10,000 regulars already there.[10]

As the line regiments and detachments arrived in the capital,
fatigued by the exertions of hasty and rapid movements, they found
that preparations for their arrival—lodging, food, equipment—were
inadequate. Furthermore, the soldiers were subjected to propaganda
which urged them to refuse to fire on their fellow citizens in order to
defend a regime that oppressed them both. Defections soon followed.
Most insubordination at this stage took the passive form of desertion;
but some soldiers indicated that they would balk at the repression of
civilians and a few threatened their superiors with violence if ordered
to perform such duty. Many officers, most importantly the military
commanders who were advising the King, were convinced that they
could not answer for the conduct of their men. As a result, virtually all
regular units in Paris were withdrawn from the city before the dramatic
events of July 14, 1789. What was lacking at this critical point was not so

---

1956), p. 135; and Albert Mathiez, *The French Revolution*, trans. by C. A. Phillips (New
York, 1964), pp. 28, 33.
    [10] On the situation in Paris in July 1789, described below, see my book, *The Response
of the Royal Army to the French Revolution* (Oxford, 1978), pp. 52-70.

much discipline as confidence on the part of the officers that they could command obedience from their subordinates. For, despite disturbing evidence of a breakdown of authority in a few units, most regular troops maintained adequate, if unenthusiastic, discipline until after the fall of the Bastille.

From this early point in the French Revolution the two major problems that were to plague the royal officer corps in the coming two years became evident. The violence of mid-July forced the King to accept the claims of the Estates General—now the self-proclaimed National Assembly—to participate in governing France under a constitution whose terms remained to be worked out. Both the monarchy and the representative legislature would share political authority; but the precise division of power was as yet undefined. As long as the Assembly and the King cooperated, there would be no serious problems; but in the event of disagreement, a very painful choice might be imposed. The second difficulty involved the relationship between the officers and soldiers. If not broken, the bonds of discipline were seriously strained; and there were ominous signs of unanticipated hostility toward officers on the part of their men. The development of these two phenomena, the ambivalent political situation and the mounting insubordination of the troops, created a dilemma for thousands of officers.

For a minority of the officer corps the limited, but fundamental, changes of the summer of 1789 were intolerable; they wasted no time in responding. A number of prominent court nobles, including the King's own brothers, determined to emigrate from France and lead a struggle against the Revolution from abroad. Most officers were either unable or unwilling to reach such a decisive conclusion during this period.[11] They awaited developments and confronted them as they occurred.

The first results of July 14 were not slow in coming. Although there had been discipline problems with some of the troops in Paris prior to the attack on the Bastille, it was only after that event that widespread insubordination became serious in these units. The desertion rate skyrocketed, attaining a level between three and four times as great as in the previous year.[12] Beyond that, as news of the crisis in Paris spread throughout the country, military insubordination accompanied it. At Rennes, Auxonne, Strasbourg, Nancy, Thionville, Bordeaux, and Caen soldiers defied their officers and displayed sympathy for the Revolution.[13] Officers were unable to counteract this. Drawn almost

---

[11] Léonard, *Armée et ses problèmes*, p. 307; and L. Hartmann, *Les Officiers de l'armée royale et la Révolution* (Paris, 1910), pp. 98, 104-107.

[12] Scott, *Response of Royal Army*, pp. 60-61.

[13] *Relation de ce qui s'est passé à Rennes en Bretagne, lors de la nouvelle du renvoi de M. Necker* [Paris, 1789]; Hartmann, *Officiers*, p. 131; Arthur Young, *Travels in France*

exclusively from a peculiar social class, performing their military service under conditions entirely different from the soldiers, and largely unaware—as well as unconcerned—with the lot of their subordinates, the noble officers were largely unprepared for such reactions from their men.[14]

The political situation tended to sanction insubordination. The National Assembly had been saved by a collapse of discipline among the troops, and so could hardly condemn it. The King, temporarily without alternatives, took a conciliatory position by offering amnesty to all soldiers who had deserted since June 1, provided they returned to their regiments by October 10.[15] Finally, civilians who encouraged and applauded insubordination furnished important support for the soldiers' actions.[16] The officers of the Royal Army were left confounded by events and without clear direction.

In the two years following the storming of the Bastille the officers' problems and confusion increased. The military changes inaugurated by the Assembly simultaneously gratified and alienated a substantial proportion of the officer corps. Although an oath of loyalty to "the Nation, the King, and the Law," required by the Assembly in August 1789, offended few noble officers, other changes were more disturbing. The abolition of feudalism, the reorganization of the Catholic Church under secular supervision, and the end of hereditary nobility alarmed many. On the other hand, pay increases and the definitive abolition of venality satisfied long-standing complaints of officers. Even the latter reform, however, aroused a mixed reaction because the same decree opened all officer ranks to all citizens, regardless of their background.[17] Under these circumstances the officers' ambivalence toward the new regime increased.

------

during the Years 1787, 1788, and 1789, ed. by Jeffrey Kaplow (Garden City, N.Y., 1969), pp. 152-54; Henri Choppin, *Les Hussards: Les vieux régiments, 1692-1792* (Paris, 1899), p. 246; Norman Hampson, *A Social History of the French Revolution* (Toronto, 1966), p. 77; and Eugène de Beaurepaire, "L'Assassinat du Major de Belsunce (Caen, 12 août 1789)," *Revue de la Révolution*, vol. 3 (January-June 1884), pp. 409-29, and vol. 4 (July-December, 1884), 26-47.

[14] Although most of the soliders' duty-time during peace was taken up by training, few officers supervised this activity. In 1788-1789, of the personnel involved in training in thirty-eight infantry and cavalry regiments, less than one in six was an officer; and these officers were mostly junior lieutenants, often officers of fortune. See the inspection reports in A.G., series X^b, cartons 14, 21, 22, 25, 26, 28, 29, 31, 33, 46, 49, 53, 58, 62, 73, 74, 81; series X^c, cartons 31, 33, 34, 35, 40, 42, 45, 47, 50, 53, 64, 72, 76, 78, 79, 81, 83; and series X^g, carton 89.

[15] Louis Gottschalk and Margaret Maddox, *Lafayette in the French Revolution, Through the October Days* (Chicago, 1969), pp. 205-10.

[16] For the role of civilian support at this point in the Revolution, see my *Response of the Royal Army*, p. 77.

[17] On the reforms, see Antoine Picq, *La Législation militaire de l'époque révolutionnaire* (Paris, 1931), pp. 305-306; and Lucien de Chilly, *Le Premier Ministre constitutionnel de la Guerre, La Tour du Pin* (Paris, 1909), pp. 283-84.

The Assembly's attitude toward the army in general and the officer corps in particular was itself ambivalent. Within the first seven months of the Revolution, the legislature carefully defined the conditions under which army units could be employed against civilians and established its control over the army's budget and organization, over promotion, recruitment, and discharge policies, and over military justice; but it left the King as its titular Commander-in-Chief.[18] The primary motivation behind these policies was the realization of the critical role played by the regular army in exercising political power. The middle-class members of the National Assembly were moderate revolutionaries who viewed the army simultaneously as a necessary bulwark against radicalism and as a potential tool of counter-revolution. They required a disciplined force for the preservation of law, order, and their own authority; yet, at the same time, they feared that the regular army might be used as a passive instrument by royalist officers opposed to the revolutionary changes. While recognizing the necessity of maintaining military discipline, they were suspicious of most officers' political loyalty.

It is difficult to analyze this loyalty over the distance of nearly two centuries. Clearly, a number of liberal nobles, many of whom had served in the American Revolution—men like Lafayette, Noailles, Custine, Ségur, the Lameth brothers—were outspoken supporters of the limited, constitutional monarchy that was emerging. Others, who emigrated from France with the princes in the immediate aftermath of July 14, 1789, just as clearly displayed their unalterable opposition to the new settlement. Most officers, however, made no political commitment. Company-grade officers with years or even decades of service probably had only a limited interest in politics. For those who were more concerned with such matters, the confusing situation and ambivalent policies of the new government prevented an unequivocal decision one way or another. In all likelihood, many officers would have been hard put themselves, even if pressed, to define precisely their own political position.

If the general circumstances neither necessitated nor facilitated a political decision, developments within the army did affect the officers' situation. Official and citizen reactions to desertions in late 1789 and early 1790 had the effect of encouraging further insubordination by the troops.[19] Like other groups in civil society, soldiers took advantage

---

[18] Picq, *Législation militaire*, p. 8; Chilly, *La Tour du Pin*, pp. 283-84; and Théodore Jung, *L'Armée et la Révolution: Dubois-Crancé (Edmond-Alexis-Louis), mousquetaire, constituant, conventionnel, général de division, ministre de la Guerre (1747-1814)*, vol. 1 (Paris, 1884), pp. 133-34.

[19] Evidence for the turmoil in the army at this time is contained in a mass of archival and secondary sources; for a summary treatment, see Scott, *Response of the Royal Army*, pp. 81-90.

of the new, unsettled atmosphere to organize political clubs and to present what they regarded as legitimate demands for the redress of grievances. Many of these claims involved the misuse of regimental funds by officers. As a result of increasing tensions, mutinies broke out in 1790 among line units garrisoned at Lille, Hesdin, Perpignan, Saint-Servan, Epinal, Stenay, Brest, Longwy, Metz, Sarrelouis, Compiègne, and Nancy.

The government's inconsistent policies fostered this unrest. On August 6, 1790 the Assembly outlawed soldiers' clubs within regiments because of their contribution to insubordination; yet, in the same decree it ordered an audit of all unit accounts, thus providing justification for the soldiers' allegations of financial malfeasance by their officers.[20] The great mutiny at Nancy, which began over the issue of regimental funds and terminated in a pitched battle at the end of August, elicited an untypically firm response from the Assembly: mutinous soldiers were executed, condemned to the galleys, or imprisoned, while two of the regiments involved were disbanded.[21] Even these measures, however, could not reverse the disintegration of the officers' authority.

Although the general revolutionary atmosphere, the ambivalent policies of the government, and the growing defiance of the soldiers all bore responsibility for the collapse of discipline, the officers themselves contributed to the problem. In spite of obvious signs of widespread insubordination, nearly half of the officer corps took their customary leave between October 1789 and May 1790, sometimes in the face of official recommendations to the contrary.[22] Such insensitivity to conditions among the troops, who were thereby left without adequate supervision during a critical time, was less excusable after the summer of 1789 than the earlier example of insubordination that many officers had given during the pre-revolutionary events of 1788. This kind of behaviour by the officers would soon exact its price.

In the last months of 1790 and the first months of 1791 a comparative, but short-lived, calm was re-established in the army. Spring, however, saw an end to this, as new incidents of insubordination occurred, for example, at Laon, Saint-Servan, and Nîmes.[23] The deterioration of

---

[20] The specific terms of this law can be found in A.G., series X^b, cartons 14, 31, and 42, as well as in the Archives départementales du Bas-Rhin, series IL, carton 1439.

[21] The most comprehensive account of the Nancy mutiny is William C. Baldwin, "The Beginnings of the Revolution and the Mutiny of the Royal Garrison in Nancy: *L'Affaire de Nancy*, 1790" (unpublished Ph.D. dissertation, University of Michigan, 1973).

[22] Information on the officers who went on leave at this critical juncture is drawn from inspection reports for thirty-four regiments (22 infantry, 11 cavalry, and 1 artillery) in A.G., series X^b, X^c, and X^d.

[23] General Biron described the incident at Laon in his letters of April 16 and 24 and May 1 and 2, 1791, contained in A.G., series B^1*, carton 208. For the trouble in Saint-

discipline convinced many officers that their situation was impossible; by the spring of 1791 some 1,200 (of a total of more than 9,400) had left the army and emigrated to join the counter-revolutionary forces that were gathering beyond the French frontiers. From their bases abroad the émigrés called upon their comrades in France to join them, by promising rewards, by appealing to their honour, and by threatening retribution.[24] Still, although confused, harassed, and intimidated, most officers remained at their posts until June 1791, when the King himself attempted to carry out a counterrevolution.

Proposals that Louis XVI should leave France dated to July 1789; specific plans for such a move began in October 1790. The indecisive monarch finally agreed to depart secretly from Paris for Montmédy near the border with Belgium, a possession of his brother-in-law, the Austrian Emperor. From this frontier town the King could rally elements of the army which were loyal to him, readily receive foreign assistance, or, failing all else, seek sanctuary across the border. The logic of the plan was impeccable, its execution abominable.[25] After failing to implement virtually every detailed arrangement, Louis XVI was finally recognized and arrested at the small town of Varennes. Upon being informed of these developments, the National Assembly ordered the temporary suspension of Louis from his functions and demanded a new oath of loyalty which omitted all mention of the King.

This was the turning point of the Revolution for the officer corps of the Royal Army. Whatever prior doubts or suspicions there may have been about the sincerity of the King's ostensible acceptance of the Revolution were confirmed. Whatever illusions there may have been about royal authority were dispelled. Louis was now a prisoner of his own subjects and the institution of monarchy itself was in grave jeopardy. While the arrest and suspension of Louis XVI constituted a crucial development for the Revolution as a whole, no single group in France was as deeply affected as the noble officers. Indeed, as the foremost authority on emigration during the French Revolution notes,

---

Servan, see the letter of the Directory of the district of Saint-Malo to the Directory of the Ille-et-Vilaine, dated May 17, 1791, in Archives Nationales (henceforth, A.N.), F⁷ 3679¹. The episode at Nîmes is described by Capt. D'Izarny-Gargas in *38ᵐᵉ Régiment d'Infanterie: Historique des corps qui ont porté le numéro 38* (Saint-Etienne, 1889), pp. 116-19, and in A.N., D xv 5, dossier 45.

[24] Donald Greer, *The Incidence of the Emigration During the French Revolution* (Gloucester, Mass., 1966), pp. 24-25; and Charles Poisson, *L'Armée et la Garde Nationale*, vol. 1 (Paris, 1858), pp. 280-81.

[25] The most useful description of the military aspects of the flight to Varennes is the articles of Michel de Lombarès, "Varennes ou la fin d'un régime (21 juin 1791)," *Revue historique de l'Armée*, no. 2 (1960), pp. 33-56, no. 4 (1960), pp. 45-62, and no. 1 (1961), pp. 23-36, as well as "Compléments à l'histoire de l'évenement de Varennes (22 juin 1791)," *Revue historique de l'Armée*, no. 3 (1971), pp. 19-37.

"1791 was essentially the year of military emigration."[26] Within two
months following the King's flight approximately 1,500 officers refused the new loyalty oath; and by the beginning of 1792 some 6,000
officers in all, nearly two-thirds of the authorized officer strength of
the line army, had emigrated from France.[27] Seldom—perhaps
never—has such a purge of so many officers taken place in such a short
time.

Clearly, the action of the King and the reaction of the Assembly
broke the last, tenuous bonds between most of the officers and the
government. Nevertheless, the situation was not as simple as this single
event seems to suggest. The sense of duty, honour, and loyalty which
had bound a substantial majority of the officer corps to the new regime
until that point was, obviously, destroyed by the flight to Varennes. But
these sentiments, whatever their importance, were intangible considerations, difficult to measure not only for subsequent historians but
even by the participants themselves. The King's attempted flight and
its failure provided incontrovertible evidence of a fundamental change
in the political system and consequently established a touchstone for
loyalty. But also, a whole series of other concrete factors, including
objectionable government policies, pressure from their peers, and
insubordination on the part of their troops, had already strained the
officers' loyalty to the breaking point. For many of them the Varennes
episode was simply "the last straw."

Yet even this important development was not sufficient to drive all
Old Regime officers from their posts; in the aftermath of the flight to
Varennes almost 3,000 noble officers continued to serve in the army. A
variety of considerations affected this decision. Some officers were
sincerely devoted to the principles and policies of the Revolution; some
remained because their loyalty to the nation superseded their commitment to any particular regime; others had a sense of professionalism that tied them to their military duties even in the most
adverse conditions; and yet others saw in the new circumstances unex-
pected opportunities for advancement. Whatever their motives, however, most officers continued to be subjected to intense pressure to
leave the army.

The King's flight set off yet another wave of clashes between
officers and soldiers; for example, at Phalsbourg, Montpellier, Blois,
Perpignan, Wissembourg, Landrecies, and Saintes. Furthermore,
these and other similar incidents displayed certain ominous trends. In
1789 and early 1790 most insubordination was passive in nature—pre-
dominantly desertion; and often during this period the soldiers had civilian
support for their conduct. Thereafter the soldiers became more bel-

---

[26] Greer, *Incidence of Emigration*, p. 25.
[27] Ibid., p. 26; and Hartmann, *Officiers*, pp. 225, 271-88.

ligerent in their relations with their officers and more willing to engage
in direct confrontations, including mutiny. At the same time, the
troops relied less on civilian support or sanction. In addition, the
N.C.O.s, who seldom participated in insubordinate activity at first,
became more prominent in such affairs from 1790; in 1791 and 1792
sergeants organized and led mutinies against their superiors. Since the
N.C.O.s filled most of the officer vacancies created by the departure of
the nobles, personal ambition neatly reinforced political commitment
to the Revolution. Finally, the struggles between officers and men
more and more frequently included charges that the officers were
politically unreliable. Noble birth was often the basis for this accusa-
tion.[28]

If all of these problems were not enough for the beleaguered
officers who stayed in the army, they also found themselves implicated
in the treason of those officers who had emigrated. Each officer who
departed increased the soldiers' suspicions of and hostility toward
those who remained. These sentiments on the part of the troops
frequently led to further insubordination, which in turn drove other
officers into emigration, thus compounding the problem. The National Assembly and the Legislative Assembly, which succeeded it in
October 1791, themselves suspicious of noble officers and uncertain of
how to deal with the army's internal difficulties, were reluctant to
restore unquestioning obedience among the soldiers and were probably incapable of doing so, had they desired. For the noble officer corps
a hopeless cycle had become established that would not end until they
had been nearly eliminated from the French army.

Developments outside the army also led to purges of noble officers. In April 1792 France went to war with Austria and Prussia. Faced
with the alternatives of fighting for the Revolution or against it, an
additional 600 officers emigrated in the following three months.[29] On
August 10, 1792 an armed crowd, composed of Parisians and National
Guard units from the provinces, overthrew the French monarchy. In
response, General Lafayette tried to turn his army against the capital;
but, having failed, he and his staff went over to the enemy.[30] Other
officers followed his example. A new round of denunciations and
attacks upon noble officers took place, contributing to yet more depar-
tures.[31] These developments affected far fewer officers than earlier
crises for the simple reason that by the latter half of 1792 most officers

---

[28] Scott, *Response of the Royal Army*, pp. 107-108, 111-12, 121.

[29] Spenser Wilkinson, *The French Army before Napoleon* (Oxford, 1915), p. 117; and
Georges Sagnier, *La Désertion dans la Pas-de-Calais de 1792 à 1802* (Blangermont, 1965),
p. 25.

[30] Marquis de Lafayette, *Mémoires, Correspondance et Manuscrits du Général Lafayette,
publiés par sa famille*, vol. 1 (Bruxelles, 1837), pp. 471-99.

[31] Scott, *Response of the Royal Army*, p. 119.

who had reservations about the new regime had already left military service. An additional factor that reduced intra-army tensions during this period was the war. In the combat zones where most regular units found themselves in the second half of 1792, the political struggles in Paris faded in significance.[32] Competent military leadership became the crucial criterion for judging officers; their political or social backgrounds were of minimal importance to the soldiers.

By the beginning of 1793 conditions in the army had settled down—temporarily. The officers corps had been substantially renovated.[33] Of the nobles who had so thoroughly dominated this organization in 1789, only about 2,000 remained in the army, constituting less than one-fourth of all the officers. Court aristocrats, who, as a group, had emigrated earliest, formed a majority only at the highest officer level—among lieutenant-generals. Provincial nobles who had withstood the pressures to leave the army now formed the largest element among the major-generals and field grade officers, ranks from which they had been effectively barred before the Revolution. While there were commoners in every officer grade, they were most numerous in the company grades; approximately three-quarters of all lieutenants and captains were of common birth and most of them had been promoted from the enlisted ranks. Regardless of their social origins, nearly all line officers were soliders with long service and had extensive combat experience. The nobles, who continued to serve as officers because of motives ranging from political conviction to personal ambition, had survived a series of intense strains on their devotion to the military service of France.

Even their obvious competence and dedication were insufficient to protect the survivors from the Old Regime against the new crises that soon developed. The military victories to which they led their forces during the fall and early winter of 1792 had forced the foreign invaders from French soil and advanced the war into enemy territory. By the spring of 1793, however, a stunning reversal of the military situation had taken place. During the winter of 1792-1793 tens of thousands of soldiers, hastily levied for the defence of the fatherland, deserted or simply went home at the expiration of their enlistment. The French supply system broke down and left troops in the field without sufficient weapons, ammunition, transport, clothing, and even food. Forced to commandeer supplies in the occupied areas, the French antagonized local inhabitants who responded with recalcitrance and hostility.

---

[32] For a participant's view of this development, see John Money, *The History of the Campaign of 1792* (London, 1794), pp. 297-98.

[33] A much more detailed description of the officer corps in early 1793 is provided in my essay, "The French Revolution and the Professionalization of the French Officer Corps, 1789-1793," in Morris Janowitz and Jacques van Doorn (eds.), *On Military Ideology* (Rotterdam, 1971), pp. 28-47.

Meanwhile the anti-French coalition recovered from the defeats of late 1792 and was reinforced by the adhesion of new allies, such as Spain, Britain, and the Netherlands. By early spring the Allies were able to launch a counter-offensive. In mid-March Dumouriez, perhaps the most able of the French generals, suffered defeat at Neerwinden and began negotiations with the Austrians. Within three weeks Dumouriez, after failing to convince his army to march on Paris, went over to the enemy.[34]

First Lafayette, now Dumouriez! The treachery of Old Regime officers was clear to all. The reaction of the government—now the democratically elected National Convention—was quick and decisive. Commissioners with ultimate authority were sent to the armies to supervise the officers and to provide for the political education of the troops. The new Minister of War, Bouchotte, himself an officer of fortune, began to purge his ministry and to compile lists of generals whose political loyalty was suspect.[35] Developments within and outside the country intensified the atmosphere of crisis. In March 1793 royalist rebellion broke out in western France. The first attempts to repress it failed completely. In June began the federalist revolts, whose manifestations took every form from official protest to violent insurrection against the central government in Paris; by August, sixty of the eighty-three departments of France were affected. Simultaneously, the French frontiers were broken by invading armies. By summer, British, Hanoverian, and Dutch troops had advanced into northwestern France; Austrian armies were besieging major fortresses along the Belgian border; Prussian forces were moving into Alsace; in the southeast the Piedmontese invaded Savoy and threatened Nice; and at both extremities of the Pyrenees the Spanish were advancing against Bayonne and Perpignan.[36] This combination of civil war and foreign invasion led the National Convention to initiate the series of extreme policies known as the Terror.

The Committee of Public Safety, elected by and among the deputies of the Convention, assumed full control of the total war effort, thereby establishing a dictatorship. The government's "representatives on mission" preempted almost all military functions from the commanders in the field, including recruitment, supply, administration, discipline, and sometimes the conduct of operations. Suspicions based on earlier experiences—notably the treason of Lafayette and Dumou-

---

[34] For a thorough account of the military situation during this period, see the following volumes of Arthur Chuquet's eleven-volume *Les Guerres de la Révolution*, vol. 2: *Valmy* (Paris, 1887); vol. 3: *La Retraite de Brunswick* (Paris, 1887); vol. 4: *Jemappes et la conquête de la Belgique* (Paris, 1890); and vol. 5: *La Trahison de Dumouriez* (Paris, 1891).

[35] Marcel Reinhard, *L'Armée et la Révolution pendant la Convention* (Paris, n.d.), pp. 79-85; and Albert Soboul, *La Révolution française*, vol. 2 (Paris, 1962), p. 113.

[36] Soboul, *Révolution française*, vol. 2, pp. 17-18.

56 *Limits of Loyalty*

riez—and fears of a military dictatorship imposed by a victorious general, determined relations between the Republic and its generals.[37] In September 1793 a "Law of Suspects" made any noble liable to denunciation, arrest, and possible execution. The Revolution, in desperate straits, demanded of its military commanders both conclusive success in combat and unquestionable political loyalty; in fact, the absence of the former requirement could be, and was, used as evidence that the latter was also lacking. Few Old Regime officers were able to satisfy both criteria.

The Terror had a devastating impact upon the officers of the former Royal Army, especially upon those who had become generals. Between May 1793 and January 1794 the Army of Italy had three different commanding generals; the Armies of the North and of the Moselle had four each; the Armies of the Western Pyrenees and of the Alps five each; the Army of the Rhine eight; and the Army of the Eastern Pyrenees had no less than eleven commanders.[38] In all, from April 1793 to July 1794 well over 300 generals were suspended, 100 were cashiered, almost 250 were arrested, and nearly fifty were executed. A large majority of the generals purged were nobles whose service dated to well before the Revolution.[39] Indeed, in April 1794 all officers of the former Royal Army were excluded by law from continuing their military service, although exception was made for those officers who fulfilled functions useful to the Republic. By mid-1794 fewer than 1,000 noble officers were still on active duty.[40]

Thus, in only five years the proportion and situation of noble officers in the army had been completely reversed. In place of 90 per cent of the officer corps, they constituted less than 10 per cent; instead of dominating its ethos, they had become a beleaguered and suspect minority. This dramatic reversal was the result of a complex series of developments which strained and eventually dissolved the ties of loyalty between the officer corps and the state.

Prior to the Revolution, various military reforms initiated by the monarchy created a general sense of dissatisfaction within the officer corps. In 1788 some officers gave striking expression of this dissatisfaction when they openly defied royal authority while ignoring the effects

---

[37] Albert Soboul, *Les Soldats de l'an II* (Paris, 1959), pp. 196-200; Jules Leverrier, *La Naissance de l'armée nationale, 1789-1794* (Paris, 1939), pp. 176-77; and Georges Michon, *Robespierre et la guerre révolutionnaire, 1791-1792* (Paris, 1937), p. 74.

[38] Ernest d'Hauterive, *L'Armée sous la Révolution, 1789-1794* (Paris, 1894), p. 314.

[39] Georges Six, *Les Généraux de la Révolution et de l'Empire* (Paris, 1947), pp. 203-26, 287; and A. C. Sabatié, *La Justice pendant la Révolution: Le Tribunal révolutionnaire de Paris* (Paris, 1912), pp. 404-405. According to Six, by the beginning of 1794 less than one-fifth of the 337 generals then serving were nobles (p. 25).

[40] Hartmann, *Officiers*, pp. 525-28; and J. Revol, *Histoire de l'armée française* (Paris, 1929), p. 134.

that such conduct might have upon their subordinates. Only when the previously quiescent Third Estate followed this example by challenging the established political order did most nobles come to see that their interests and those of the monarchy were inextricably bound together. They rallied to the King; but in doing so they were committing themselves to a regime that would soon be fundamentally altered. Ultimately, the royal officer corps would share the same fate as the Old Regime, of which it was an integral part.

Generally speaking, the distinct groups that composed the pre-revolutionary officer corps reacted differently to successive stages in the process of political transformation brought about by the Revolution. At the same time, their reactions significantly affected this process. The highly placed court aristocrats wanted to preserve the Old Regime in its totality and refused to accept the changes that resulted from the events of the summer of 1789. They formed the first wave of émigrés and provided early evidence for distrust of the nobility.

The majority of officers—provincial nobles—reacted to the mixed regime that was emerging with an equivocal attitude that was matched by the Assembly's ambivalence toward them. A series of policies enacted by the new legislature antagonized many nobles and taxed their political allegiance. Simultaneously, mounting insubordination by the soldiers, which the Assembly was unwilling or unable to halt, threatened their military authority. These developments gradually strained their devotion to duty, until the flight and arrest of the King destroyed what remained of their loyalty to the state. They emigrated *en masse* after mid-1791, thus further undermining public confidence in the noble officers who continued to serve. Further emigration and treason on the highest military levels, together with the dual crisis of civil war and foreign invasion in 1793, changed the government's attitude toward noble officers from ambivalence and suspicion to intolerance and hostility. During the Terror it became almost impossible for noble officers, regardless of their services, to convince the revolutionary authorities of their loyalty.

In contrast, the ex-rankers, who had been victimized by social prejudice before 1789, were the primary beneficiaries of the radical changes that opened to them unprecedented opportunities for professional dignity and advancement. With each wave of emigration these experienced soliders became more essential to military policies of the government which, in turn, rewarded them with numerous and rapid promotions. Officers like these—e.g., Hoche, Pichegru, Bernadotte—provided the skill and devotion that led the armies of the Republic to victory.

Not all officers followed this pattern. Some court nobles, like Lafayette, served in the army until the overthrow of the monarchy; and a few, like Lauzun, commanded armies as late as 1793, although virtually none survived the purges of the Terror. While the suspension of Louis XVI in 1791 was obviously a turning point for most of the lower nobility, every phase of the Revolution between 1789 and 1794 led to the alienation of some provincial aristocrats. On the other hand, even the Terror failed to drive hundreds of these officers from the army. Conversely, some commoners who received commission before or during the Revolution rejected the new regime and voluntarily emigrated.[41]

Despite some valid generalizations, then, there is no single or simple explanation for the varied responses of the royal officer corps to the French Revolution. A number of factors determined the eventual results; the officers' perception of the state, the government's attitude toward and treatment of the officers, conditions within the army, the general political atmosphere, pressures from peers, changes in the military situation, and personal peculiarities all played a role. Indeed, this should not be surprising since loyalty is a complex and dynamic relationship, rather than a simple, static sentiment. In a period of substantial and rapid change, when loyalty is a most critical consideration, it is, unfortunately, most difficult to determine.

---

[41] A very striking example of such behaviour is provided by two officers of fortune, Pichon and Sirjacques, of the Lauzun (6th) Hussars; these officers, who had both served in the United States during the American Revolution, went over to the enemy in August 1792. See Gilbert Bodinier, "Etude du comportement des officiers qui ont combattu en Amérique, pendant la Révolution," a paper presented at the 102ᵉ Congrès national des Sociétés savantes at Limoges in April 1977, a copy of which Capt. Bodinier has kindly given me.

PATRIOTS FOR ME: OBSERVATIONS ON THE HABSBURG PROFESSIONAL OFFICER CORPS, 1868-1918

GUNTHER E. ROTHENBERG

IN HIS influential study *The Soldier and the State*, Huntington postulated that the change from mercenary and aristocratic officership to professionalism was the result of the crisis of the Napoleonic wars and he further suggested that this "was virtually always associated with the shift in the rank and file from career soldiers to citizen soldiers."[1] But this statement must be modified. Professional officership—corporate unity, career structure, and training—date back at least to the mideighteenth century and, except for Russia, the European powers had made only marginal and temporary adjustments to meet the Napoleonic challenge. The Austrian rulers especially felt that conscription threatened the position of absolute monarchs and for the fifty years after 1815, they retained, as far as possible, an army on the traditional eighteenth-century pattern of aristocratic officers and long-serving professional troops, strictly regimented and isolated from the rest of society.[2] And with the maintenance of internal security as its major task, such an army served the needs of the empire until it was defeated decisively in 1866 by Prussian conscript armies.

The lost war had enormous political and military consequences. Bowing, albeit reluctantly, to the new realities, the Emperor Francis Joseph came to an accommodation with liberal sentiments and the most obstreperous and powerful national minority in his empire, the Magyars. The famous Compromise of 1867 replaced the Austrian Empire with the Dual Monarchy of Austria-Hungary, two distinct constitutional monarchies joined by one ruler—Emperor of Austria and King of Hungary. In addition there were certain common or "joint" institutions, including the ministries of war, finances, and foreign affairs. Joint budgets were voted on separately by two parliaments, in Vienna and in Budapest, and had to be renegotiated every ten years. This arrangement gave Hungary's normally unified politicians considerable leverage, especially in military appropriations, though the Vienna Parliament—representing not only Austrian Ger-

---

[1] Samuel P. Huntington, *The Soldier and the State* (New York, 1964), pp. 37-39.

[2] Gunther E. Rothenberg, "The Austrian Army in the Age of Metternich," *Journal of Modern History*, vol. 40 (1968), pp. 155-65.

mans, but also Czechs, Slovaks, Poles, and others—also could prove difficult.

A new and difficult era began for the "joint" imperial-royal army. In fact, military affairs had proved so intractable during the Compromise negotiations that they had to be settled in a separate agreement the following year. At first the Hungarians had insisted on a separate national army for the Kingdom, though in the end they accepted the continuation of the "joint" army and the establishment of two second line forces—the Austrian *Landwehr* and the Hungarian *Honvéd*. The emperor-king retained control over the joint army, subject to budgetary restraints, while the second line units were directed by separate defence ministries. In addition, Hungary consented to the introduction of conscription throughout the entire monarchy, a portion of the annual recruit intake going directly into the national formations. This complicated solution, however, did not settle the issue. The Hungarians continued to press for a truly independent national army, while parliamentarians in Austria resented imperial command prerogatives and the dynastic orientation of the military establishment.[3] As a result, while appropriations for the separate forces were adequate, and in the case of the Hungarians even lavish, the joint army, the one most visible and vital instrument of unity in the divided monarchy, found itself starved of funds and manpower. These shortcomings, manifesting themselves in fewer divisions, reserves, and outdated equipment became dramatically evident in 1914.[4]

But the most immediate and complex problem of the joint army, and we are concerned with this force which employed the overwhelming majority of professional officers, was national diversity, reflecting the problems of a divided state, national dissensions, and a manpower base fluctuating widely in skills, literacy, and combat spirit. According to official count there were 267 Germans, 223 Hungarians, 135 Czechs, 38 Slovaks, 85 Poles, 81 Ruthenes, 26 Slovenes, 67 Croats and Serbs, 64 Romanians and 14 Italians for every 1,000 men in its ranks.[5] This not only created difficulties in communications, but in an age of growing national aspirations and resentments it represented a

---

[3] Gunther E. Rothenberg, "Towards a National Hungarian Army: The Military Compromise of 1868 and its Consequences," *Slavic Review*, vol. 31 (1972), pp. 807-12.

[4] The statement by Norman Stone that "the weakness of the Habsburg Army in 1914 stemmed not from the disaffection of its soldiers but from the intransigence of politicians in Hungary," is one summation. "Army and Society in the Habsburg Monarchy, 1900-1914," *Past & Present*, no. 33 (1966), p. 103. A German military observer commented that "the Danubian monarchy and its army were adequately prepared for a campaign against Servia but not for a war against the major European powers." August von Cramon, *Unser österreichisch-ungarischer Bundesgenosse im Weltkrieg*, 2nd rev. ed. (Berlin, 1922), p. 200.

[5] *Militärstatistisches Jahrbuch für das Jahr 1913* (Vienna, 1914), p. 147.

danger to the spirit of the army itself. This was recognized by its leaders and by civilian observers. Already in 1855, Friedrich Engels had commented that "no one can predict how long this army will stay together," and in 1895 Count Casimir Badeni, Austria's prime minister, remarked that a "state of nationalities can not make war without danger to itself."[6] High-ranking officers regularly echoed these sentiments. "All preparations for foreign war," Conrad von Hötzendorf, Chief of Staff for the "entire armed forces" of the monarchy wrote in 1906, "are useless as long as our internal situation is not resolved."[7] Conrad referred here both to the threatening situation in Hungary, which the year before had brought the Dual Monarchy to the brink of civil war, and to the ever more violent struggles of the other nationalities.

And yet, things were not as black as they seemed. As severe a critic as the Hungarian liberal Oscar Jászi conceded that until the very end, the joint army remained a "school of loyalty and a stronghold of unitary sentiment," while an English commentator found in 1913 that the army constituted a "constant corrective to particularist ambitions."[8] Another observer conceded that serious problems existed, but asserted that the army remained effective. "The maintenance of unitary sentiment and of efficient organization in this maze of languages and races," he observed, "is a dynastic and military miracle—a miracle accomplished by the devotion of its corps of officers."[9]

Often regarded as vast impersonal organizations, armies do appear to manifest specific characteristics, reflecting not only the societies that raise them, but their own corporate standards set largely by their officers. The rank and file normally has little influence and, provided there are good officers, effective fighting units have been formed from the most unpromising recruits. This seemed to be substantiated by the performance of the Austro-Hungarian army in World War I. Although it entered into its last war lacking national cohesion and unprepared for fighting on the scale of 1914-1918, Liddell Hart pointed out that it stood the test for over four years "in a way that surprised and dismayed [its] opponents."[10] And if there is any credit in this it belongs above all to the professional Habsburg officer corps which, facing considerable difficulties in coping with the problems of a divided state, national dissensions, social unrest, and a multinational manpower base fluctuating widely in literacy and combat spirit, nonetheless was able to

---

[6] Cited in Arthur J. May, *The Hapsburg Monarchy, 1867-1914* (Cambridge, Mass., 1951), p. 491.

[7] Cited in Oskar Regele, *Feldmarschall Conrad* (Vienna, 1955), p. 81.

[8] Oscar Jászi, *The Dissolution of the Habsburg Monarchy* (Chicago, 1929), p. 142; O.T.C., "The Austrian Army," *Westminster Review* (February, 1913), p. 122. Cf. R. W. Seton-Watson, *Racial Problems in Hungary* (London, 1908), p. 256.

[9] Henry Wickham Steed, *The Hapsburg Monarchy* (London, 1914), pp. 61-62.

[10] Basil H. Liddell Hart, *The Real War 1914-1918* (Boston, 1930), p. 39.

train an army whose record has been unjustly slighted. The purpose of this article then is to explore certain aspects of this remarkable body of men; there is no intention to argue the case either for or against the Habsburg monarchy or to provide a thumbnail sketch of the army's history during the period. This has been done elsewhere.[11]

As it emerged after 1868, the Habsburg professional officer corps bore the imprint of the reforms introduced a century earlier by Empress Maria Theresa and continued by her son and co-ruler Joseph II. Finding on her accession an officer corps from a wide spectrum of society, foreign as well as Austrian, and patently lacking the homogeneity provided in the Prussian service by the *Junker* class, the empress attempted to provide this by attracting a larger proportion of the native aristocracy into the service. When this attempt failed, largely because the Theresan reforms also had removed financial incentives from military careers, she opened up entry into the officer class to all qualified men and decided to compensate them by elevating their social status. She decreed that all officers be admitted to her court and that commoners be ennobled after thirty years of good service. Continued and expanded by her successors, these practices introduced an important new component into the officer corps: a service nobility, for the most part landless and of middle class origin, which identified itself with the dynasty, served it for generations, and became in the words attributed to Emperor Francis "patriots for me."[12]

The progress of this service nobility and non-aristocratic officers in general, was uneven. If by 1815 already over 20 per cent of serving generals belonged to these classes, the next forty years saw a resurgence of well-connected, aristocratic amateurs, especially in the higher command echelons. This tendency was reversed by the debacle of 1859, blamed by many, in and out of the army, on the incompetence of aristocratic commanders. Thus on the eve of the war with Prussia in 1866, the service nobility again held about 20 per cent of all general officer slots, and a higher percentage of court and courtesy appointments are discounted. Even more important, during a period when modern technology increasingly became a determinant military consideration, the specialist officers of the general, engineering, and artillery staffs were almost entirely drawn from the service nobility and the bourgeoisie.[13]

After 1868 this trend continued and accelerated. The increased size of the army, the ever greater role of technology, and the ever more

---

[11] Gunther E. Rothenberg, *The Army of Francis Joseph* (W. Lafayette, Ind., 1976).

[12] The exact origin of this famous statement is hard to trace. It frequently appears in the literature, among others in Jászi, *The Dissolution*, p. 142.

[13] Gunther E. Rothenberg, "Nobility and Military Careers: The Habsburg Officer Corps, 1740-1914," *Military Affairs*, vol. 40 (1976), pp. 182-84.

important necessity to provide for fast mobilization demanded highly trained professionals. The service nobility and commoners came to predominate in the officer corps. As early as 1878 they constituted 58 per cent of all generals, and by the outbreak of World War I they dominated all branches and commands. The nominal head of the mobilized army was a member of the imperial house, Archduke Friedrich, but the real commander was the Chief of Staff, Conrad von Hötzendorf, who was only one generation removed from the bourgeoisie. And out of 14 corps commanders only three could be considered members of the aristocracy; the remainder were service nobles or commoners. Even the so-called "feudal" cavalry regiments no longer were aristocratic preserves; out of 42 commanding officers in 1914, only nine were aristocrats.[14]

This development had been helped along by the abolition in 1868 of the appointment and promotion prerogatives of the regimental proprietors, now a purely honourary title, and by the introduction of branch-wide promotion criteria in 1875. No longer tied to social criteria, the most important determinant of an officer's career was his method of entry. Disregarding the medical, judicial, veterinary, administrative, and chaplaincy branches, there emerged three basic career patterns: the dynastic, the academic, and the cadet. The dynastic was, of course, reserved for members of the imperial house who normally were commissioned at fourteen and after serving briefly as subalterns, received a staff or nominal command position which rarely interfered with their other pursuits. To be sure, there were exceptions like Archduke Albrecht, the Emperor's great-uncle, a good field commander, and Inspector General from 1869 until his death in 1896. The dynasty always would maintain an important and perhaps often unfortunate influence on appointments to high command, but below that level it rarely exerted any influence on careers.[15]

The overwhelming majority of officers followed the academic or the cadet career patterns. The so-called *Akademiker* were graduates of the two military academies—the Theresan Military Academy and the Technical Military Academy. Normally commissioned at twenty, they formed a self-conscious elite with a definite edge in obtaining the best postings. However, with only about 200 graduates a year, the academies could not meet army requirements and the majority of professional officers, about three-fifths of the annual intake, came from fifteen cadet schools throughout the Dual Monarchy. Compared to the academy graduates, cadets received an inferior education and faced limited career prospects. Upon graduation they were not commissioned at once but entered the service as cadet officer deputies and

[14] Ibid.
[15] Rothenberg, *Army of Francis Joseph*, pp. 81-83.

received the golden sword knot—the symbol of commissioned rank—only after several years of probationary duty. Though there was no statutory barrier to their advancement, few cadets reached senior rank. Most served their careers at company or battalion level, passing quietly into retirement as captains or majors.[16] But their contribution to the army was considerable. They provided the cadres of long-service, small-unit commanders giving cohesion and continuity to their formations.

Overall, the Austro-Hungarian service took on a middle-class cast. Its style was modest; few regiments boasted splendid mess silver or luxurious officer quarters. Increasingly, officer candidates came from the families of serving officers, lower-rank civil officials, and the petty bourgeoisie. "Aristocrats of birth, property or intelligence," a cavalry officer complained in 1874, "no longer can be found among the younger generation of officers."[17] His sentiments were echoed between 1908 and 1910 by General Moritz von Auffenberg who worried that the constantly declining social character of the corps made it difficult to attract "desirable" candidates. He admitted that little could be done to induce the high aristocracy to follow military careers, but asserted that because of the unique role of the army in safeguarding the dynasty, special efforts should be made so that the "officer's calling would once again become the magnet for the middle and higher strata of society."[18]

Auffenberg, a close confidant of Archduke Francis Ferdinand, the heir apparent, expressed apprehension that the changing social composition of the corps, combined with the low pay scales, might tempt young officers to listen to socialist agitation. On the other hand, he was confident that nationalist dissidence—the gravest internal threat to the monarchy—was not a problem within the career officer corps.[19] Unlike the men in the ranks, the corps did not represent a national cross section of the monarchy. While Germans constituted only 24 per cent in the general population, they provided 791 out of every 1,000 officers. The remainder consisted of 97 Magyars, 47 Czechs, 23 Poles, and 22 Croats and Serbs.[20] The low number of Magyars—20 per cent of the general population but less than 10 per cent of career officers—

---

[16] Ibid. Cf. Johann C. Allmayer-Beck, "Die Allzeit Getreuen," in Heinz Siegert (ed.), *Adel in Österreich, Probleme, Fakten, Analysen* (Vienna, 1971), pp. 311-12, and Allmayer-Beck, *Die k.(u.)k. Armee 1848-1914* (Munich-Vienna, 1974), pp. 175-76.

[17] Ibid., p. 176.

[18] Austria, Kriegsarchiv Wien, Nachlass Auffenberg, 1910, MS., "Geist und innere Verfassung der Armee," pp. 5-12.

[19] Ibid., 1908, MS., "Über die Verfassung des Offizierskorps und die Stimmung in demselben," pp. 11-16.

[20] *Militärstatistisches Jahrbuch für das Jahr 1905* (Vienna, 1906), pp. 144-46. Discussion in Rothenberg, *Army of Francis Joseph*, pp. 127-28, 151.

reflected nationalist feelings in Hungary and not a bias against their entry. As a liberal Hungarian critic of the monarchy conceded, the joint army "stood both in principle and in practice on the basis of national equality."[21] And the Hungarian officers who did select military careers in the joint army, as opposed to those in the *Honvéd*, shared the general legitimist feelings of the corps. In 1903, when the Hungarian government succeeded in obtaining the privilege for officers of Hungarian citizenship to transfer to Hungarian regiments, more than 1,000 officers opted for Austrian citizenship.[22]

The heavy preponderance of Austro-German officers should, moreover, not be considered as denoting an ethnic or national allegiance. German in the military context denoted allegiance to the spirit of the entire monarchy, the *Gesamtstaat*, as against the separatist aspirations of the various national groups. In effect the joint army and, above all, its officer corps, constituted a state within a state where the concept of a great and united empire headed by an emperor-king was translated into reality. The poet Grillparzer had proclaimed in 1848, "In deinem Lager ist Österreich!" and the joint army officer corps maintained this tradition. It even used its own language, the *ärardeutsch*, a strange officialese scorned by the literati, and it retained a few international aristocratic soldiers who found their national origins not incompatible with absolute loyalty to the imperial-royal warlord. For instance, the Inspector General of Engineers in the 1880s was Feldmarschall Leutnant Daniel Baron Salis-Soglio, a Swiss, who when approached by his native government for expert advice on new alpine fortifications, formulated the classic reply that "As a Swiss I would be delighted to do this, but as an Austrian officer I cannot oblige without His Majesty's permission."[23]

The reply illuminated the overall orientation of the corps. Officers rarely identified with any particular region of the monarchy or with their ethnic background. They served everywhere, from the mountains of the Tyrol to the plains of Galicia, in large cities and small hamlets, their life regulated by the daily routine and their home wherever the black-yellow imperial standard flew. Socially isolated and only too well aware that their pay scales and living standards were below that of the higher civil service, the Austro-Hungarian officer compensated by creating a self-image as the defender of the dynasty, a member of a noble elite separate and far above the self-seeking landed

---

[21] Jászi, *The Dissolution*, p. 143.

[22] Theodor von Sosnosky, *Die Politik im Habsburgerreiche*, vol. 2 (2nd ed.; Berlin, 1913), p. 204.

[23] Daniel Freiherr von Salis-Soglio, *Aus meinem Leben*, 2 vols. (Stuttgart, 1908), vol. 2 p. 108.

aristocracy and the money-grubbing middle classes. Habsburg officers rejected the managerial concept of officership. As Colonel Angeli expressed it before the turn of the century: the uniform and the traditions of the service set the soldier apart from other men and the officer's calling could not be measured in economic terms, but by his special conceptions of honour.[24] The Habsburg officer corps was loyal to the emperor-king, proud of branch and regiment, and maintained this attitude amid the ever more violent quarrels of nationalities and classes marking the last decades of the Dual Monarchy.

The officer corps maintained its posture of steadfast loyalty, albeit with some internalized misgivings and fears, at the price of isolating itself from society at large. But this, of course, was not to be expected from the reserve officers and the rank and file who increasingly were influenced by nationalist and socialist agitation. Senior officers were apprehensive about the ultimate effects of these tendencies and by 1913 were prepared to deal with the growing problems of nationalist and socialist disaffection by the old expedient of stationing troops outside their home districts.[25] It is, however, worth noting that these fears were not shared abroad. A German general staff memorandum of 1913 declared that the Habsburg officer corps still constituted the "main and at this time quite effective counterbalance against the polyglot character of the army" and that the troops still were "disciplined, willing, patriotic, largely loyal to the emperor and not yet touched by anti-military agitation."[26] An English observer was even more complimentary to the officer corps. "Perhaps what strikes the foreign observer most forcibly," the military correspondent of the *Westminster Review* noted in 1913, "is the admirable feeling existing between officers and men. This general spirit of *camaraderie* ... is in striking contrast to the sharp lines of division that freeze off confidence between the various ranks in the German army." The correspondent attributed this to two reasons. First, "the average Austrian recruit is in natural intelligence greatly superior to the average German recruit," and secondly, the "average Austrian regimental officer ... does not treat his men like numbered units, but generally takes the trouble to know them individually."[27]

Such complimentary views were, of course, exaggerated and certainly not universal. Otto Bauer, an Austrian socialist leader who served as a reserve officer during World War I, presented an opposite view. Relations between the Prussian soldiers and their *Junker* officers,

---

[24] Moritz von Angeli, *Aus dem Nachlass* (Vienna, 1905), pp. 84-86.
[25] Discussed in Rothenberg, *Army of Francis Joseph*, pp. 170-71.
[26] Cited in Alfred Vagts, *A History of Militarism* (New York, 1937), p. 273.
[27] O.T.C., "The Austrian Army," pp. 122-23.

he claimed, actually were closer than those between the Austrian troops and their middle-class officers. The *Junker*, because of their established positions, commanded natural respect while the Austrian officer had to buttress his position by artificial means.[28] The evidence, in short, is contradictory. But if combat performance is considered the supreme test of the work of an officer corps, then the Habsburg officers passed the test with flying colours. Of course, the army suffered defeat, but victory or defeat against great odds is not the prime criterion for judging combat performance as German, French, Japanese, and Confederate examples attest. What matters is how well an army stands up to prolonged combat stress, and here the Habsburg army did as well as any other belligerent force in World War I. Writing some fifty years later, and from a perspective much more detached than contemporary or near-contemporary observers, Professor Zeman concluded that the Habsburg army "remained an effective instrument until the summer of 1918 . . . and the balance sheet . . . in the four years of war speaks in its favor."[29]

So far, this essay has emphasized the positive aspects of the Habsburg officer corps, but there were stresses beneath the surface. To be sure, the ultimate allegiance of the officer corps to the emperor-king never was in serious doubt, though relations between the dynasty and the officer corps—and especially the senior soldiers—were troubled by several major issues, in part interrelated. The first was that unlike its German counterpart, the Habsburg officer corps never occupied the first place in state and society. While the army constituted an important support for the dynasty—after 1867 it was one of the few institutions functioning in both halves of the divided monarchy—it never became separate from, or achieved superior standing to, the political authorities. As A. J. P. Taylor observed, the Habsburg empire never became a *Militärstaat* in the Prussian sense. In fact, "the 'military monarchy' of the Habsburgs was the least militarized state in Europe."[30] Although the army still presented itself with much glitter and panache and the emperor habitually wore its uniform, he never confused an institution of the dynasty with the dynasty itself. Soldiers never were as highly regarded as senior civil servants and their advice regarding solutions for internal and external difficulties facing the state was often ignored.

The officers knew this and they resented it. As Feldmarschall Leutnant Blasius von Schemua, interim Chief of Staff in 1912, wrote,

---

[28] See his introductory remarks in O. Bauer, *Die Offiziere der Republik* (Vienna, 1921), pp. 2-5.

[29] Z. A. B. Zeman, *The Break-up of the Habsburg Empire* (London-New York, 1961), p. 39.

[30] A. J. P. Taylor, *The Habsburg Monarchy 1815-1918* (New York, 1965), p. 229.

the empire was in a period of waning authority and rising discontent. Threatened by powerful external enemies, its internal situation was equally dangerous. The old values were no longer respected and everywhere in the monarchy "subjects are rebelling against the government which no longer stands firm but merely tries to appease selfish interests." Amid this growing chaos, Schemua asserted, only the officer corps retained a sense of mission and commitment to the entire state, yet soldiers were poorly rewarded. Their pay, so the general complained, was well below that of the civil service, and civilian ministers and officials received more consideration and honours from the emperor than did his loyal soldiers.[31] An even more bitter note was struck after the war by Conrad, widely regarded as the model of the ever-loyal Habsburg soldier. Writing in his private notebook he concluded that since the days of Maria Theresa the Habsburg rulers had lacked all martial qualities and that the last two rulers, Emperor Francis Joseph and especially Emperor Charles, had done absolutely nothing for the army and had scandalously neglected deserving officers.[32]

Of course, this was written in the bitterness of defeat and while Conrad was suffering his last, fatal illness; but since 1867 there had been several major clashes between the soldiers and the emperor, his dynastic representatives in the army, and his civilian ministers. These conflicts were not always clear cut and on several occasions the military representatives of the dynasty in the army sided with the soldiers. Oversimplified, these conflicts involved the structure and orientation of the army, and military demands for more forceful action against internal and external enemies, imagined or real.

The first clash between senior officers and the dynasty, represented between 1868 and 1895 by the Inspector General, Archduke Albrecht, erupted in the early 1870s. The archduke, as well as almost all senior generals, had been opposed to the military concessions made to Hungary and to parliamentary controls. Only an imperial fiat had brought them into line. But once the new order was established there was a clash, both personal and on principle, between the new joint war minister, Feldmarschall Leutnant Franz Baron Kuhn, a German liberal

[31] Austria, Kriegsarchiv Wien, "Militärpolitische Denkschrift angangs 1912," Generalstab Op. B. F-95. Cf. Alfred Krauss, *Die Ursachen unserer Niederlage* (Munich, 1920), p. 72. Complaints by soldiers about the preeminence of civilian officials were, of course, common in the Habsburg monarchy. In 1848, for example, Field Marshall Radetzky commented that the army had no reason to love the former absolute regime. "It was, if you want to call it despotism," he wrote, "a civilian and not a military despotism which neglected and deprived the army." Radetzky to Baillet de Latour, September 30, 1848, Kriegsarchiv Wien, Hofkriegsrat, Präsidial Reihe Nr. 216.

[32] Kurt Peball, ed., *Conrad von Hötzendorf. Private Aufzeichnungen* (Vienna, 1977), pp. 192-93.

from Bohemia who wanted to build the new army on the French pattern of ministerial responsibility, cooperating if necessary with Parliament; and the archduke, who wanted to keep the army as a dynastic instrument and reduce ministerial and parliamentary influence as far as possible. The quarrel split the officer corps into opposed "court" and "ministerial" factions which openly attacked each other in military journals. In the end the minister lost, both because the emperor supported the archduke and because, mistakenly regarding the general staff as a stronghold of aristocratic privilege, Kuhn tried to reduce its position. This, however, provoked Colonel Friedrich von Beck, then head of the imperial military chancery and an advocate of a powerful general staff. Beck, a clever diplomat and a close associate of the emperor, managed to topple Kuhn by a temporary alliance between himself, Albrecht, and Gyulai Andrássy, Hungary's powerful foreign minister. The latter was drawn into the conflict both because of Kuhn's continued opposition to expansion of the *Honvéd*, ironically an objective also close to the heart of Albrecht, and by Kuhn's open advocacy of Austro-Hungarian intervention in the Franco-Prussian War. In the end, lacking a substantial base, the war minister had to resign in 1874 and his successors never held much power or influence. The staff was expanded and after a decent interval of seven years, Beck emerged as the next Chief of Staff.[33]

Albrecht for that matter also did not care much about staff work; he had the aristocrat's disdain for the "quill pushers," but Beck managed to conciliate him and for the next two decades the two men directed the Habsburg army along lines which were neither "liberal" in the jargon of the time—that is directed towards permitting either the war minister or Parliament a major role, nor purely dynastic. As far as the officer corps was concerned, however, the trend was definitely in the direction of a dynastic legitimist orientation, unavoidable perhaps because of the continuing, and after 1888, escalating conflict with Hungary.

From the outset, the military settlement of 1868 had not been entirely satisfactory. Military men continued to regard the *Honvéd*, deliberately cast in the image of the revolutionary army of 1848-1849, as a potential danger, while Hungarian nationalists regarded it merely as a stopgap towards a completely independent national army. However, despite occasional clashes between loyalist officers of the joint army and Hungarian extremists, the settlement muted differences for the next twenty years. Beginning in 1888 the situation changed. Although under the Compromise arrangements the Budapest govern-

---

[33] Rothenberg, *Army of Francis Joseph*, pp. 79-80, 89, and 106, and Allmayer-Beck, *Armee*, p. 178.

ment and Parliament had little influence over the internal affairs of the
joint army, they could exert considerable weight during the decennial
renegotiations of the army and the recruit quotas. The joint army bill of
1889, which aimed to increase the army slightly, led to stormy scenes in
the Budapest Parliament and rioting in the streets. It passed only after
Vienna made important concessions, the most important perhaps a
symbolic change in the title of the joint army from *k. k. Armee* to *k.u.k.
Armee*.[34]

The struggle over the conjunction *und* seems trivial, but it was
considered by the leadership of the joint army as one of several deliber-
ate steps ultimately leading to severing of the bonds of the military
establishment. For this reason the army command, and even Emperor
Francis Joseph, always conciliatory towards the Magyars, opposed the
next Hungarian demand: the introduction of the Magyar "language of
command" in all units of the joint army recruited in the Kingdom of
Hungary, regardless whether they were ethnically Magyar or not. The
"language of command" consisted of some eighty German drill
phrases, learned mainly by rote; the joint army also recognized ten
different regimental languages for the conduct of the routine business
and instruction within a unit. In fact, few units were monolingual. The
majority had two, and a substantial minority had three and even four
regimental languages which officers were required to master. But the
German language of command was considered absolutely essential, not
so much as a means of communication but as the symbol of the unity of
the joint army. And for just this reason the Magyars insisted on this
change.[35]

When early in 1903 the joint war minister proposed a rather
modest increase in the recruit quota to keep step with the growing
population, Hungarian nationalist radicals refused their assent unless
their demands for the Magyar language of command were met. At first
it appeared as if Francis Joseph would stand firm, but then he caved in
and made substantial concessions, though he stood fast on the language of command question. However, these conciliatory steps did not
resolve the issue and unrest continued and even escalated in Hungary.
By 1905 there was near chaos. No taxes were collected; no recruits were
levied. Deeply perturbed, the joint army's general staff prepared
"Operation U": armed intervention in Hungary with reliable units.
Though detailed plans were worked out and troops were ready to
move, the emperor drew back at the last moment and made additional
concessions.[36] He preserved the German language of command but at

---

[34] Ibid., pp. 119-20.

[35] Ibid., pp. 119, 131-37. For a graphic view of the linguistic diversity see
Allmayer-Beck, *Armee*, pp. 130-32.

[36] Kurt Peball and Gunther E. Rothenberg, "Der Fall 'U'. Die geplante Besetzung

the price of permitting the *Honvéd* to assume in all essential aspects the character of a national army.[37] Even so, the pattern of Hungarian demands and imperial accommodation continued until 1912, when temporarily satisfied (though the issue would be raised again in 1917), the Hungarian Parliament began to vote additional appropriations and manpower for the joint army. Convinced that his policy had been correct, Francis Joseph told Conrad that "after all, the Magyars are a reliable element."[38]

Most senior soldiers would not agree. Soon after Conrad took office in 1906 he had urged strong action. He stressed that it was "intolerable that the very existence of the army is constantly threatened by the refusal of the Hungarian Parliament to provide recruits and money."[39] He constantly pressured the emperor to stand firm against Hungarian demands and just as constantly found himself overruled. Other prominent generals echoed his sentiments. "Every strengthening of the army, every improvement," wrote General Krauss, "had to be bought from Hungary."[40] One young staff officer, Captain Kerchnawe, took the unusual step of taking the military case, albeit anonymously, to the public. In a widely circulated pamphlet he described a future war in which the Dual Monarchy, fatally weakened by Hungarian sedition, socialist agitation, and dithering by the government, found itself attacked and overwhelmed by an Italian, Russian, Serb, Montenegrin, and Bulgarian coalition, with Germany standing by and merely occupying Bohemia to protect her own security.[41] The future would, of course, be different. When war came, the *Honvéd* proved loyal and its morale high. Yet, in a period when all the other European powers were arming feverishly, the obstruction of Magyar politicians had cost the army heavily and talk about the "withering away of the army" was not without substance. Some ten years later a thoughtful German observer of the Austro-Hungarian army, General Hans von Seeckt, wrote in a confidential memorandum that "even before the war, the hopelessness for a thoroughgoing reform had sapped military energies."[42]

Ungarns durch die k.u.k. Armee im Herbst 1905," *Schriften des Heeresgeschichtlichen Museums in Wien*, vol. 4 (1969), pp. 85-125.

[37] Bundesministerium für Landesverteidigung, *Österreich-Ungarns letzter Krieg*, 7 vols. (Vienna, 1930-38), vol. 1, pp. 27-29. For the Hungarian demands in 1917 see Regele, *Conrad*, pp. 439-41 and the documents in Kriegsarchiv Wien, Militärkanzlei seiner Majestät 1918, 38-2/1,2.

[38] Franz Graf Conrad von Hötzendorf, *Aus meiner Dienstzeit*, 5 vols. (Berlin, 1921-1925), vol. 3, pp. 84-86.

[39] Ibid., vol. 1, pp. 503-505.

[40] Krauss, *Die Ursachen*, p. 63.

[41] [Hugo Kerchnawe], *Unser letzter Kampf* (Vienna-Leipzig, 1909), passim.

[42] Militärarchiv Freiburg, Nachlass Seeckt, Nr. 247/32, f. 26-27.

The necessary thorough reforms would, of course, have required a complete restructuring of the Dual Monarchy, something well beyond the horizon and the capabilities of the army which regarded itself as the "mute servant of the dynasty." Some officers hoped for improvement after Archduke Francis Ferdinand, the heir apparent, who was known to have far-reaching plans for restructuring the Dual Monarchy, ascended the throne. Others, and they included, above all, Chiefs of Staff Conrad and Schemua, looked for a solution by preventive war. Recognizing that the army was weak and most likely would become weaker relative to the prospective enemies, Conrad repeatedly urged the emperor to wage preventive war either against Serbia or Italy, or for that matter against both, while Austria-Hungary still could do so with a good chance of success. As Conrad wrote in his memoirs: "During my peacetime tenure as chief of the general staff I realized that the very existence of the Monarchy was threatened. But my opponents either discounted these dangers or believed that a policy of patience would diminish them. I, however, was convinced that they could only be removed by preemptive action."[43]

There is no need to narrate these often described events again in detail. Like most professional soldiers and military intellectuals of his day, Conrad believed that relations between states were in a permanent, open or latent, state of conflict, that war therefore was inevitable, and that there was practically no difference between aggressive and defensive wars. It was the Chief of Staff's duty to choose the most favourable time for starting a war and only such a well-chosen stroke would restore the waning prestige and the unity of the Dual Monarchy.[44] It was a heady brew, but Francis Joseph, and his Foreign Minister Count Aehrenthal, refused to go along with the proposition that in formulating foreign policy likely to lead to war under any circumstances, "the responsibility of the Chief of Staff is far greater than that of the foreign minister."[45]

Conrad's continual pressure for war constituted a direct challenge to the emperor's policy and on November 15, 1911, he was summoned to the palace and informed by Francis Joseph that "my policy is peace and everyone must conform to it."[46] A fortnight later he dismissed Conrad and demoted him to Inspector of Infantry. For the moment the civilians had prevailed but Schemua, Conrad's successor, shared his attitudes. As a result, with the Balkan War in progress, Conrad, widely,

[43] Conrad, *Aus meiner Dienstzeit*, vol. 1, p. 13.
[44] Peball, *Conrad*, pp. 91, 188. Cf. Solomon Wank, "Some Reflections on Conrad v. Hötzendorf based on Old and New Sources," *Austrian History Yearbook*, vol. 1 (1965), pp. 75-88.
[45] Rothenberg, *Army of Francis Joseph*, pp. 144-45.
[46] Ibid., pp. 163-64.

though perhaps mistakenly, considered the foremost strategist in the army, was returned to his former post in December 1912. He immediately renewed his call for armed action only to be overruled once again by the emperor.[47]

By this time, moreover, Conrad's relations with Francis Ferdinand had soured. For all his belligerent rhetoric, Francis Ferdinand had inherited the Habsburg habit of caution and was unwilling to chance the existence of the dynasty on the uncertain fortunes of war. He wanted to use the army for internal consolidation. Although he had only a sketchy military education and his brief service with troops had not been a success, the archduke had been appointed Inspector General of the Armed Forces in 1913 and had no qualms about mixing in internal army affairs. As a devout, even fanatic Catholic, he objected to Conrad's handling of the Redl affair in which a colonel, found to have sold mobilization plans to Russia, was induced to commit suicide to avoid the embarassment of a trial. An open clash between the two men occurred during the autumn 1913 manoeuvres when, without bothering to inform the Chief of Staff, Francis Ferdinand changed manoeuvre dispositions. In the argument that followed, the archduke hinted that Conrad should be careful not to become another Wallenstein and the incident was papered over only with difficulty.[48] On this unhappy note ended the last year of peace, perhaps symbolizing the strained relations between the officer corps and the dynasty.

The performance of the Habsburg army during World War I was, as already has been stated, well above expectations. Although it entered the war with a fatalistic sense of disaster—Conrad wrote to a friend that it would be "a hopeless struggle, but it must be because such an ancient monarchy and such an ancient army cannot perish ingloriously"—it did surprisingly well.[49] Mobilization went well and fears regarding nationalist disaffections proved, at least temporarily, without foundation. To be sure, within the first few months of the conflict it emerged that strategic dispositions had been faulty and training and equipment outdated.[50] Insistence on the offensive brought heavy casualties, which by the end of the first year changed the character of the army. With casualties of three-quarters of a million men during the first six months, and losses especially heavy among regular officers and men,

---

[47] Ibid., pp. 168-69.

[48] Karl F. Nowak, *Der Weg zur Katastrophe* (Berlin, 1919), p. 153. The incident probably was embellished by Nowak who became Conrad's close friend during the war years.

[49] Conrad's letter in Gina Gräfin Conrad von Hötzendorf, *Mein Leben mit Conrad von Hötzendorf* (Leipzig-Vienna, 1935), p. 114. For his second thoughts on the prospects of war see Peball, *Conrad*, p. 166.

[50] Rothenberg, *Army of Francis Joseph*, pp. 177-86.

"the old regular army died in 1914," in the words of the official history. It became a mere skeleton, fleshed out with hastily mustered conscripts, recalled regular officers, newly graduated academicians and cadets, and reservists—"essentially a militia force."[51] Still, the remaining regulars and the old traditions, especially a widely shared sense of legitimate obedience owed to the aged emperor, helped to hold this under-trained and poorly equipped force together.

Moreover, there was astonishing recuperative capacity. The Dual Monarchy managed to replenish its ranks, procure new weapons, and withstand the attack of another major enemy, Italy, in the spring of 1915. While armament and supply always remained well below the level provided by the major industrialized belligerents, the Austro-Hungarian combat soldier, *Kamerad Schnürschuh* as the Germans called him, had little in common with the fictional Private Schwejk. He adjusted to modern combat conditions, learned to assault and defend, and above all to endure and to persist fighting in offensives all too often planned by staffs too far removed from the front and too remote from actual conditions.[52] While performance of the Austro-Hungarian higher commands, from the supreme command down to corps level, left much to be desired (though as much can be said of the other belligerents), lower level unit commanders often were excellent and held the army together.

Although a serious blow, the army even survived the death of Francis Joseph in 1916; but his successor, Archduke Charles, never commanded much respect and was, correctly as it turned out, suspected by senior officers of being willing to end the war on any terms. Shaken by the death of the "old emperor" and by the losses sustained on the Russian front in the summer of 1916, the army began to show the strains of war by the winter of 1916-1917. There were increased signs of military disintegration, mutinies, defections, and desertions, but much still depended on individual commanders, and the army as a whole remained a viable instrument into the summer of 1918 when the failure of a poorly-planned offensive against Italy deprived it of its last hope.[53]

By the late summer of 1918 signs of a breakdown of the military establishment were clearly evident. Even so, the Austro-Hungarian army still clung to its lines in Italy, stood deep in Russia, and conducted a fighting retreat in the Balkans. But the war was lost and the end came

---

[51] *Österreich-Ungarns letzter Krieg*, vol. 2, p. 271.

[52] Among others see Kurt Peball, "Führungsfragen der österreichisch ungarischen Südtiroloffensive im Jahre 1916," *Mitteilungen des österreichischen Staatsarchivs*, vol. 31 (1973), p. 423.

[53] On the conception, execution, and consequences of this operation see Peter Fiala, *Die letzte Offensive Altösterreichs* (Boppard, 1967).

on October 16, 1918 when Emperor Charles conceded to the various nationalities the right to form their own states. Followed within days by an imperial decree releasing officers from their oath of allegiance and permitting them to join the forces of these new states, this action destroyed the last bonds of legitimacy and obedience. Under these circumstances it is truly amazing that when on October 28 the long-awaited enemy offensive in Italy begun, *k.u.k.* units still fought back for a number of days. By October 30, however, Czech, Hungarian, Croatian, and finally even Austro-German units, refused to go into action and demanded to be sent home. Some Tyrolean regiments, directly defending their homeland, resisted until November 2, but that was the end, except for the isolated Balkan army of General Pflanzer-Baltin which did not cease fighting for several more days.[54]

Against all expectations and prognostications, the army had fought for almost four and a half years. The most fragile and internally divided army, badly handled by its supreme command and poorly equipped, had held out just as long, and in some cases even longer, than more homogeneous forces. There were mutinies and desertions, but nothing on the scale of the Russian or French mutinies of 1917; at the end, there was a loss of will to fight, but this was true just as much of the German ally who so often scorned the performance of the Habsburg ally. Of course, as Conrad once noted after the war, all European nations displayed extraordinary staying powers throughout the war. Few, however, had expected that the complicated, ramshackle and bitterly divided Habsburg Monarchy and its army could do so. Looking back more than forty years later, an Austrian historian concluded that, lacking national cohesion and faith in ultimate victory, the army had put up a good fight based on "good regimental spirit and comradeship. It fought for the honour of the flag, for its superiors, and perhaps even to earn a decoration."[55] These qualities had been the values cherished by the Habsburg professional officer corps, which paid the price with 13.5 per cent of its total numbers lost in action, compared to 9.8 per cent casualties suffered by reserve officers and troops.[56]

There have been speculations whether a different and more effective solution to the military problems of the Dual Monarchy could have been found. Andreski, a military sociologist, asserted that in an era of rampant nationalism the wisest course for the Dual Monarchy would have been the retention of an old-fashioned professional army. The

---

[54] Rothenberg, *Army of Francis Joseph*, pp. 215-18. The various interpretations concerning the consequences of the imperial manifesto and the question of the military oath are discussed in Oskar Regele, *Gericht über Habsburgs Wehrmacht* (Vienna-Munich, 1969), pp. 155-58.

[55] Heinrich Benedikt, *Monarchie der Gegensätze* (Vienna, 1949), p. 195.

[56] Anton Wagner, *Der erste Weltkrieg* (Vienna, 1968), pp. 316-17.

introduction of conscription, he maintained, was a mistake.[57] On the other hand, a prominent Austrian military historian has held that the army relied far too much on dynastic sentiment and tradition and that this prevented it from gaining wide-based, popular support. Kurt Peball suggested that a truly multinational army, perhaps on a federal basis, would have been most appropriate for the Dual Monarchy.[58]

Personally, this author disagrees with both alternatives. By 1868 the dynamics of liberalism and nationalism had destroyed any realistic prospects for continuing an eighteenth-century-style army. Moreover, long before 1914 it was accepted by all the states of continental Europe that the military effectiveness on which they relied to preserve their relative power and status depended not on small professional forces but on a combination of skilled professional soldiers with the entire human, economic, and moral resources of the population. At the same time, clashing national aims and rising antagonisms, something over which the army had little influence, effectively doomed any prospects for an Austro-Hungarian army founded on military particularism. To the degree that national and social conflicts in the Habsburg Empire could not be solved by political means—and it is worth noting that these antagonisms persist to this very day in the successor states despite radical changes in regimes—they could not be solved by the army. Under these conditions the traditionalist and conservative orientation of the officer corps appears as the only viable option. In the end the qualities of courage, leadership, and devotion to duty were not enough to save an empire whose existence had become an anachronism; but it is to the credit of the officers that they tried.

---

[57] Stanislav Andreski, *Military Organization and Society* (Berkeley-Los Angeles, 1968), p. 70.

[58] Kurt Peball, "Sendung und Erbe," in *Österreichische Militärische Zeitschrift*, Spec. Issue 1966, pp. 59-61.

THE LIMITS OF LOYALTY: FRENCH CANADIAN OFFICERS AND THE FIRST WORLD WAR

DESMOND MORTON

Trois éléments indispensables constituent une nation; la populace, le térritoire, et la marine. Le couronnement de l'édifice est la force militaire. Aucun peuple ne saurait prétendre au titre de nation s'il n'a chez lui un élément militaire.[1]

THUS IT was that Sir George-Etienne Cartier introduced the first Militia Bill of the young Dominion of Canada in 1868. Well aware of the fragility of the new Confederation and of the diverse military experiences of its sometimes reluctant citizens, Cartier intended to be the architect of a truly unifying national institution.[2]

Half a century later, Cartier's institution passed a glorious test. Led for the most part by officers trained in the militia, the four divisions of the Canadian Corps advanced in line on the Easter weekend of 1917 and captured Vimy Ridge. It was an achievement from which, in Ernest Renan's famous phrase, nations are made. However, Canada in 1917 was more deeply divided in national consciousness than at any time in its history. For more than two million Canadians, the salient event of 1917 was not an impressive military victory but a collective humiliation. In French Canada, 1917 was the year of Conscription.

For the majority in Canada, World War I had become a national crusade. For a minority, it was a wasteful diversion of lives and resources. There could be no compromise between these views. Crusading is incompatible with patient tolerance. Whether they believed they were saving Britain, serving the Empire, making the world safe for democracy, or achieving national regeneration through suffering, the opinion makers of English Canada could tolerate no slackening of the war effort. The terrible casualty lists, eventually totalling 60,000 in a population of only seven million, only hardened their resolve.

For most French Canadians the war evoked at most a dutiful sympathy, best illustrated by the episcopal statements which first appeared on September 23, 1914. For most French Canadians, appeals to

---

[1] Joseph Tassé, *Discours de Sir Georges Cartier, Baronnet, accompagnés de notices* (Montreal, 1893), p. 566.

[2] See Desmond Morton, "French Canada and the Canadian Militia," *Histoire Sociale/Social History*, vol. 3 (April 1969), pp. 32-35.

rescue Britain and even France were irrelevant. Criticism and sneers from English-speaking politicians and editors provoked bitter resentment, not guilt. A fearless, tireless campaign against the war effort, led by Henri Bourassa and his *nationaliste* allies became a catalyst and eventually an expression of that resentment.[3] Finally, on the Easter weekend of 1918, condemned and deserted by their own leaders, ordinary people in Quebec City launched their own brief rebellion against the Military Service Act.[4]

French Canadians were not unanimous. By the spring of 1917, 14,100 French-speaking Canadians—8,200 of them from Quebec—had joined the Canadian Expeditionary Force (C.E.F.).[5] Their officers came, for the most part, from the same community of young, educated French Canadians who had proved most responsive to the arguments of Bourassa and the *Ligue nationaliste*. Unlike Colonel Armand Lavergne, who proudly boasted that he would not desert the battle of the Franco-Ontarians against Regulation 17, French Canadian officers had abandoned the national cause "pour une aventure quelque peu interessante en pays étranger."[6]

In the circumstances, the limits of the loyalty of French Canadian officers were tested many times. Unlike their English-speaking comrades, they could count on little enthusiasm from those they had left behind. To soldiers in the Canadian Corps, the Conscription election of December 1917 could be interpreted as a commitment to their continued support; that commitment was not echoed from Quebec.[7] Even within the Corps, French Canadians found themselves in an alien, English-speaking environment. Outside the protective environment of their own 22nd Battalion, they could easily encounter (or imagine) insults, prejudice, and oppression.[8]

---

[3] On French Canada and the First World War: Elizabeth Armstrong, *The Crisis of Quebec, 1914-1918* (New York, 1937); Robert Rumilly, *Histoire de la Province de Québec* (Montreal, n.d.), vols. 19-23 passim; Jacques Michel, *La participation des Canadiens français à la grande guerre* (Montreal, 1938), and a recent synthesis, Gérard Filteau, *Le Québec, le Canada et la guerre, 1914-1918* (Montreal, 1977).

[4] Noted by Fernand Dumont in the introduction to Jean Provencher, *Quebec sous la loi des mésures de guerre, 1918* (Trois Rivières, 1971).

[5] Canada, House of Commons *Debates*, June 25, 1917. Some higher estimates ignore non-French Canadians in Quebec battalions. Even a tenth of the 22nd Battalion in 1915 was in this category. See P.A.C. Kemp Papers, vol. 119, file 16.

[6] *Le Devoir*, November 22, 1915, cited by Rumilly, *Québec*, vol. 20.

[7] Evidence of French-speaking participation different from other military voters was not discovered although Laurier's agent in England recruited scrutineers from the French-speaking 150th Battalion at Witley. See Desmond Morton, "Polling the Soldier Vote: The Overseas Campaign in the Canadian General Election of 1917," *Journal of Canadian Studies*, vol. 10, no. 4 (November 1975).

[8] See, for example, the experience of Arthur Lapointe, *A Soldier of Quebec, 1916-19* (Montreal, 1931), p. 20 and passim.

It is easy to argue that French Canadians met the test of loyalty and passed it brilliantly. The evidence of Courcelette, Regina Trench, and Cherisy, where every officer of the 22nd Battalion was killed or wounded, should be sufficient testimony. While discipline problems in the French Canadian battalion are suggested by the fact that it contributed five of the twenty-five Canadians executed by firing squad during the war, no record exists of officers of the 22nd failing in their loyalty.[9]

However, in the circumstances of the C.E.F., the question and the answer may both have to be altered. Unlike professional officers, who must face altered political circumstances during a career, officers in the Canadian Expeditionary Force had to choose their role. Those who accepted Bourassa's arguments could, like Colonel Lavergne, refuse to serve. In Quebec, as C. G. Power recalled, those who enlisted were not heroes "nor did staying at home bring white feathers."[10]

The appropriate test to put to the French Canadian militia was how far it was able to provide suitable officers even for the limited numbers of French-speaking volunteers from Quebec. The answer would be far less reassuring. The responsibility lay as much with prewar Canadian militia policy as with the events and misadventures of the wartime years.[11] A military organization which had to turn to officers like Colonel Louis-H. Archambault of the 41st, Colonel Onésime Readman of the 167th, or Colonel Tancrède Pagnuelo of the 206th Battalion had failed disastrously in a test it should have been able to pass.

The Canadian militia of 1914 had to turn to such men because of structural failures which stretched back to Cartier and his way of creating a national institution. For him, and for successors like L. F. R. Masson and Sir Adolphe Caron, it was enough that the French fact should be suitably represented in the force and its administration. Two out of three military districts in Quebec had French Canadian staff officers although the senior officer at Montreal for a decade was a

---

[9] R.G. 24, vol. 2538, HQS 1822-2. See Desmond Morton, "The Supreme Penalty: Canadian Deaths by Firing Squad in the First World War," *Queen's Quarterly*, vol. 79, no. 3 (Autumn 1972), p. 349. Only one officer in the C.E.F., a French Canadian, was ever cashiered for desertion in the face of the enemy. He was sentenced to ten years' penal servitude, remitted at the end of the war. R.G. 9, file 10-12-50-2. Like other aspects of military discipline, further research is prevented by Department of National Defence restrictions.

[10] Norman Ward, ed., *A Party Politician: The Memoirs of Chubby Power* (Toronto, 1966), p. 42.

[11] For a more extended argument, see Desmond Morton, "French Canada and War, 1868-1917: The Military Background to the Conscription Crisis of 1917," in J. L. Granatstein and R. D. Cuff (eds.), *North American Society and War* (Toronto, 1971), pp. 84-103.

well-connected politician who knew no drill.[12] In 1872, when artillery
schools were authorized to replace the departed British garrison, most
of the officers and half of the men in the battery at Quebec were French
Canadian. One of three infantry schools approved in 1883 was desig-
nated to serve the French-speaking militia.

Representation was remembered when the militia was employed
on active service. One of the two Canadian battalions sent to the Red
River in 1870 was commanded by French Canadians. In 1885 two
battalions from Quebec joined in the North-West campaign. In 1899
senior French Canadian officers were carefully included in the official
contingents organized for the South African War.[13]

Concern about representation was a political response to a structural problem. Across Canada, both English- and French-speaking
militia units shared many problems in the post-Confederation years.
Defence spending was limited. Arms, uniforms, and equipment were
worn out. Only private funds could buy the new uniforms, the band
instruments, and the lively social life that attracted recruits. In
English-speaking communities, militia officer rank brought sufficient
status and prestige that wealthy men could be persuaded to absorb the
costs of the smarter city regiments. Outside Quebec, with its garrison
traditions, where militia social life "faisait la pluie et le beau temps," no
such situation prevailed in French Canada.[14]

Despite Cartier's intentions, the Canadian militia remained a
faithful if sometimes burlesque imitation of a British model, from its
uniforms and drill to the complex customs of the officers' mess. Occasional British generals like Ivor Herbert and Edward Hutton might
remind their Canadian subordinates of the value of bilingualism but
the language of the militia was English.[15] Out of the brief two-week
militia camp, complained Armand Lavergne, it took three days before
the French Canadian militiamen could understand the commands.[16]

In the absence of community support, their own traditions and
language, and of any perceived external threat, French Canadians
could still find a few reasons for becoming militia officers. As elsewhere
in the Dominion, there were political advantages in the prominence of
militia rank and there was the opportunity to deliver small favours.

---

[12] A. C. de Lotbinière-Harwood to Sir John A. Macdonald, January 12, 1887,
P.A.C., Caron Papers, vol. 194, ff. 5775-76.

[13] Morton, "French Canada and the Militia," pp. 34, 42, 47.

[14] On the status of officers, see Jean-Yves Gravel, *L'Armée au Québec: un portrait
social, 1868-1900* (Montreal, 1874), p. 68.

[15] Morton, "French Canada and the Militia," pp. 44-46.

[16] Armand Lavergne, "National Defence as viewed by French Canadians," lecture
delivered at the Canadian Military Institute, November 19, 1910. See also *Canadian
Military Gazette*, September 26, 1911.

Humbler voters welcomed the chance to earn even fifty cents a day at camp. To the indignation of the commandant of the military school at St-Jean, militia commanding officers persisted in sparing local tax-payers by sending misfits and ne'er-do-wells to spend a winter in barracks.

Because the position of French Canadians in the militia was se-cured by *ad hoc* political arrangements and not by fundamental institu-tional recognition of legitimate needs and traditions, the eventual reform of the force in the 1890s proved devastating. Despite a tradition of French-speaking ministers and officials in the Militia Department, despite linguistic enclaves in the staff and permanent force, the train-ing, administration, and official values of the Canadian militia had remained British. Political considerations which overlooked ignorance or inefficiency for the sake of representation were not repudiated.[17]

Militia reformers like Generals Herbert and Hutton and Lord Dundonald were bilingual and conscious of French Canadian concerns, but their zeal to eliminate old, incompetent, and corrupt officers always seemed to find more scope in Quebec than elsewhere. Permanent force officers, including able French Canadians, were sent to England to perfect their military knowledge. Increasingly, a professional military career meant divorce from cultural and linguistic roots. Colonel Oscar Pelletier, son of the Liberal Speaker of the Senate and a wounded veteran of Paardeberg, retained his Quebec roots through his father's influence.[18] Colonel François Lessard, who commanded the Royal Canadian Dragoons in South Africa, virtually cut his ties with French Canada and was best known in Toronto equestrian circles.[19]

The Royal Military College, opened in 1876, was the first Cana-dian military institution to pay no attention to special French Canadian needs. Its first commandant, Colonel E. O. Hewitt, refused to com-promise standards for French-speaking applicants. As a result, of the first 1,000 ex-cadets, only thirty-nine were French Canadians.[20] One of them, Thomas-L. Tremblay, survived a near-total lack of English and the culture shock of coming from Chicoutimi to Kingston. Later, he commanded the 22nd Battalion in action, won promotion to

---

[17] Morton, "French Canada and the Militia," pp. 44-49.

[18] O. C. C. Pelletier, *Mémoires, souvenirs de famille et récits* (Quebec, 1940), pp. 175-300 recalled the experience of a French Canadian officer in British military schools. The militia, Pelletier recalled, was "une galère où la politique joue les premiers vid ons."

[19] On Lessard, J. F. Cummins, "A Distinguished Canadian Cavalry Officer," *Cana-dian Defence Quarterly*, vol. 3, no. 2 (January 1926). For a more hostile view of Lessard, see Rumilly, *Québec*, vol. 22, pp. 63-64; or Sir Sam Hughes, Canada, House of Commons *Debates*, February 1, 1917, p. 368.

[20] R. A. Preston, *Canada's R.M.C.: A History of the Royal Military College* (Toronto, 1969), p. 70.

Brigadier-General and was undoubtedly the most successful French Canadian soldier in the field.[21] There were few who shared his background and his preparation.

By 1914 the militia in Canada could look back on twenty-five years of almost unbroken reform, growth, and rearmament. In too many respects, the French Canadian component had been left behind. Since 1899 a militia staff course had prepared officers for senior appointments in time of war. By 1913 only seven of the fifty-eight graduates were French speaking. In 1913 one of four brigadier-generals and three of the twelve colonels in the permanent force were French Canadian but only twenty-seven of a total of 254 officers. It was in the middle ranks, where wartime advancement would come, that representation had become dangerously thin.[22]

Efficiency and professionalism diminished the impact of crude patronage politics in the force, and time had reduced the numbers and influence of the militia lobby—the parliamentary colonels who had once formed an impressive bloc in the Canadian House of Commons.[23] However, unlike members of a professional officer corps, militia officers did not even try to escape political debate, particularly in the pre-1914 period when defence questions mattered as much as they had in the 1860s.

The years before 1914 saw the climax of that combination of imperialism and Canadian nationalism which Carl Berger has described in *The Sense of Power*. Not only did the movement embody a strong current of ideological militarism but it also helped to confirm a new role the militia had discovered in 1899.[24] In addition to strike duty and the unlikely prospect of a new round of the War of 1812, the militia now might participate in an expeditionary force should Britain again become engaged in a major war. Others might shrink from such a practical consequence of imperialism; militia enthusiasts could embrace it eagerly.

In French Canada, some aspects of militarism, such as the cadet movement, struck a surprisingly responsive chord.[25] Imperial military expeditions did not. "Our duty as Canadians and as part of the Em-

---

[21] J.-H. Chaballe, *Histoire du 22ᵉ bataillon canadien-français*, vol. 1: *1914-1919* (Montreal, 1952), pp. 351, 353.

[22] Morton, "French Canada and the Militia," pp. 48-49.

[23] Desmond Morton, "The Militia Lobby in Parliament: The Military Politicians and the Canadian Militia, 1868-1897," in Adrian Preston and Peter Dennis (eds.), *Swords and Covenants* (London, 1976), passim.

[24] Carl Berger, *The Sense of Power: Studies in the Ideas of Canadian Imperialism, 1867-1914* (Toronto, 1970), particularly chap. 10.

[25] Desmond Morton, "The Cadet Movement in the Moment of Canadian Militarism, 1909-1914," *Journal of Canadian Studies*, vol. 13, no. 2 (Summer, 1978).

pire," Lavergne told the Military Institute in Toronto, "is to build up a strong Canada by preparing in Canada a strong national defence."[26] The assertion was not cheerfully received; nowhere did the *nationalistes* reflect Quebecois opinion more accurately.

These opinions would have mattered less if they had not, thanks to an extraordinary coalition of opposites, led to the defeat of the Laurier government in 1911. The new Conservative administration of Sir Robert Borden included fervent Anglo-Canadian imperialists in the same cabinet as Quebec *bleus* and *nationalistes* who owed their election to Bourassa.[27]

There was never much doubt which element would prevail. Borden's French Canadian colleagues preferred cabinet solidarity to their election pronouncements. At once both Bourassa and the Quebec Liberals set out to undermine them. The Quebec ministers' position was further weakened because of their impotence to protect Franco-Ontarians from the Conservative government of Ontario and Regulation 17. Never had French Canadian representation at Ottawa been more feeble or discredited.[28]

For militia officers in Quebec, the change of government had two consequences. Perhaps even more than officers elsewhere, they tended to be open partisans and to play the patronage game. In 1913, his career damaged by deafness and loss of political leverage, Colonel Pelletier resigned.[29] His successor was Colonel J. P. Landry, former commanding officer of the 61st Regiment de Montmagny and, by convenient symmetry, son of the new Conservative Speaker of the Senate. In turn, Landry's appointment allowed Bourassa's lieutenant, Armand Lavergne, to become a colonel.

Taking staff jobs from permanent officers and giving them to militia enthusiasts was only one of many reforms forced through by Borden's Minister of Militia, Colonel Sam Hughes. Never had Canada known a minister of such unbridled energy, self-confidence, and aggression. Hughes made no secret of his belief that every able-bodied Canadian should be taught to shoot and that the armouries should become the recreation centre for each town. Until the recession of 1913 Hughes was fairly popular in English-speaking Canada. Militia officers

---

[26] Lavergne, "National Defence," p. 102.

[27] R. C. Brown, *Robert Laird Borden: A Biography*, vol. 1: *1854-1914* (Toronto, 1976), pp. 188-208; Armstrong, *Crisis of Quebec*, pp. 86-87.

[28] See Filteau, *Le Quebec*, pp. 20-23. On Ontario, see Rumilly, *Québec*, vols. 19-20; Margaret Prang, "Clerics, Politicians and the Bilingual Schools Issue in Ontario, 1910-1917," *Canadian Historical Review*, vol. 41, no. 4 (December 1960); Marilyn Barber, "The Ontario Bilingual Schools Issue: Sources of Conflict," *Canadian Historical Review*, vol. 47, no. 3 (September 1966).

[29] Pelletier, *Mémoires*, p. 370.

grumbled when he banned beer and liquor from camps and messes, smirked when he publicly scolded permanent force officers, and rejoiced in the growth in organization, equipment, and training of the force.[30]

It was a measure of Hughes's sensitivity to French Canada that he claimed that his Huguenot ancestry gave him special understanding of French feelings. An outspoken Orangeman and almost a caricature of the "imperial-nationalist," Hughes soon could also be portrayed as an enemy of the French-speaking militia. In June of 1914 he peremptorily forbade the 65th Carabiniers Mont-Royal to march in the traditional Corpus Christi procession. After a storm of protest he allowed them to march without arms.[31] A few weeks later he stopped the 17th Regiment de Levis from escorting the newly-promoted Cardinal Begin. For units whose role in religious ceremonies was one of the few links with community feeling, Hughes's directives were humiliating and demoralizing.

In peacetime Hughes could do his party little good and his country little irreparable harm. In war, when the militia system was put to serious test, he could be a national disaster.

Two years earlier plans had been prepared for the kind of mobilization the European war entailed. A division of infantry and a brigade of cavalry, based on the existing militia and carefully balanced for regional and national representation, was available.[32] The Minister had known of the plan, had ignored it and, when it was needed, scrapped it. Mobilization was managed his way, with hundreds of telegrams to militia officers and cronies, orders and counter-orders, a whirlwind of confusion and chaos with one man supremely responsible at the centre.[33]

Of the 36,000 men who appeared at Valcartier, 1,245 claimed French origins and just over 700 came from Quebec's French-speaking militia units.[34] In Montreal, the 65th Carabiniers contributed one-quarter of the men in a composite unit which would become the 14th

---

[30] C. F. Winter, *Lieutenant General Sir Sam Hughes: Canada's War Minister, 1911-16* (Toronto, 1931); S. H. S. Hughes, "Sir Sam Hughes and the Problem of Imperialism," *Historical Papers* (1950), pp. 30-40.

[31] *La Presse*, June 18, 1914; P.A.C., R. L. Borden Papers, OC 190, pp. 15614-19. The 65th had begun as an escort for the Bishop of Montreal. See Ernest Chambers, *Histoire du 65e Carabiniers Mont-Royal* (Montreal, 1906), p. 72.

[32] On the plans, see A. F. Duguid, *Official History of the Canadian Forces in the Great War, 1914-1919*, General Series, vol. 1: *Appendices* (Ottawa, 1938), p. 12.

[33] See G. W. L. Nicholson, *Canadian Expeditionary Force, 1914-1919: Official History of the Canadian Army in the First World War* (Ottawa, 1962), pp. 18-28.

[34] Duguid, *Official History, Appendices*, pp. 56-58. For a valuable history of military manpower problems in both world wars see J. L. Granatstein and J. M. Hitsman, *Broken Promises: A History of Conscription in Canada* (Toronto, 1977).

Battalion of the Canadian Expeditionary Force.[35] Men from other French regiments were clustered in the 12th Battalion, together with volunteers from New Brunswick and Prince Edward Island. When, in due course, the 1st Division went to France, the 12th Battalion was left behind as a reinforcement unit. French Canada's representation was limited to a single company of the 14th Battalion. The only senior French Canadian officer was Lieutenant-Colonel H. A. Panet of the Royal Canadian Horse Artillery.[36]

To Hughes this would have seemed a matter of supreme indifference. Quebec had its representation in Richard Turner, the Victoria Cross winner who commanded the 2nd Brigade. Hughes was not alone. In London, the Colonial Secretary had passed on a suggestion that Canada might raise a "Royal Montcalm" regiment to associate Quebec with "an Empire War." George Perley, the acting Canadian High Commissioner and Member of Parliament for Argenteuil-Two Mountains, sent the notion to Borden without endorsement: ". . . personally doubt wisdom of doing anything to accentuate different races as all are Canadian."[37]

The consequences of Hughes's attitude proved disastrous for the ambitions of French Canadian officers and the pride of French Canada. Within weeks of entering the line, the 1st Canadian Division won renown for its role at the second battle of Ypres. From its ranks would come most of the commanders of subsequent Canadian brigades and divisions. The qualifications of men who had won their experience in battle had to take precedence over those whose training was gained in peacetime manoeuvres and whose rank depended on the Minister's favour. The tiny handful of French Canadian officers in the Division gained advancement but most of them were fated to return to Quebec for the humiliating struggle to recruit compatriots for the front.[38]

Within weeks French Canadian exclusion from the prominent appointments in the First Contingent had become a grievance in Quebec.[39] Dr. Arthur Mignault, a wealthy pharmaceutical manufacturer and surgeon of the 65th, offered $50,000 to raise a French Canadian battalion for the Second Contingent.[40] After a delegation of fifty-eight prominent Quebec politicians and businessmen travelled to Ottawa to lobby Borden, the proposal was accepted.[41] On October 15,

[35] R. C. Featherstonehaugh, *The Royal Montreal Regiment* (Montreal, 1927), pp. 4-7.
[36] Morton, "French Canada and War," p. 96.
[37] Perley to Borden, August 8, 1914, P.A.C., Perley Papers, vol. 1, f. 12.
[38] Of six officers in the original French Canadian company of the 14th Battalion, three became lieutenant-colonels.
[39] Rumilly, *Québec*, vol. 19, pp. 32-33.
[40] Mignault to Borden, September 25, 1914, Borden Papers, OC 209, p. 21272.
[41] Ibid., pp. 21281, 21284; Chaballe, *22e bataillon*, pp. 21-23.

1914, 15,000 Montrealers gathered at the Parc Sohmer to hear Sir Wilfrid Laurier launch the recruiting drive with the ritual invocation of Dollard Desormeaux.[42] According to Mignault, more than 5,000 recruits rushed forward in the following weeks.[43] The officers, including a future governor general, represented many of the historic leading families of French Canada.

That was not the full story. Already Bourassa had abandoned his early support for the war effort. The Parc Sohmer rally was dismissed in *Le Devoir* as "chauvinisme creux et stérile." "Retrouvons nos têtes," he commanded.[44] Organizers boasted that the new battalion had mustered 900 men: the nominal rolls showed only 27 officers and 575 men. By the time the 22nd Battalion left Canada on May 20, 1915, it had diverted recruits from other Quebec units and had absorbed a final draft of 100 men.[45] Long before Bourassa's campaign against the war could have penetrated beyond the educated elite, it should have been obvious to the government and to the Militia Department that voluntary recruiting in French Canada would face extraordinary difficulties.[46]

In addition to the 22nd Battalion, a second belated gesture had been made to French Canadian sensibilities: Colonel J. P. Landry was given command of a brigade. However, shortly before the 2nd Canadian Division left England for France, its commander, Major-General Sir Sam Steele, and two brigadiers were replaced by officers from the 1st Division. It was inevitable. Steele was far too old; Landry and his fellow brigadier were too inexperienced to take men into action.[47] In Quebec, Landry's military competence would not be questioned. Instead, the brigadier's removal was interpreted simply as an act of political vengeance. His father, Senator Philippe Landry, had taken command of the Franco-Ontarian resistance to Regulation 17. Sam Hughes had struck back.[48]

That was a measure of Quebec's priorities in 1915. "Si l'on nous demande d'aller battre pour l'Angleterre," Lavergne had declared at the outbreak of war, "nous répondrons: Qu'on nous rende nos écoles."[49] For Bourassa, opposition to the growing war effort rested on a

---

[42] O. D. Skelton, *The Life and Letters of Sir Wilfrid Laurier*, vol. 2 (Toronto, 1921), p. 437.

[43] Mignault to Borden, July 7, 1917, Kemp Papers, vol. 63, p. 2.

[44] Rumilly, *Québec*, vol. 19, p. 64.

[45] Duguid, *Official History, Appendices*, pp. 344-45.

[46] Pelletier had given warning as early as 1912. See ibid., p. 12.

[47] On Landry, see Borden Papers, OC 414, pp. 43456ff.; Perley to Borden, June 14, 1915; Perley Papers, vol. 4, f. 89.

[48] Rumilly, *Québec*, vol. 20, pp. 99-100.

[49] Ibid., vol. 19, p. 21.

complex interpretation of Canada's obligations within the British Empire; other *nationalistes* found it simpler to lay the *Boches* of Ontario against the *Boches* across the Atlantic.[50] Among the German atrocities was the attempt to rob little Alsatian children of their French language and culture. Were the Irish Catholics and Protestants of Ontario any less guilty?

Elsewhere in Canada, the Ontario school issue was treated as an absurd or a disgraceful diversion from the national crusade. In Ontario, voters had settled the issue with massive unanimity in the 1914 general election. The western provinces were already following suit by dismantling French-language education. In Ottawa, Borden and his colleagues rejoiced that the issue was solely in the provincial jurisdiction and buried themselves deeper in the war effort.

The recruiting methods for the C.E.F. were appropriate to a national crusade. Only volunteers, Hughes insisted, would be worthy to serve in such a holy cause. Married men must have written consent from their wives before they could enlist. Politicians, businessmen, and militia colonels vied for the honour of raising battalions. County councils raged if their district was ignored. Black and Japanese Canadians pleaded for the right to demonstrate their patriotism.[51] By the end of 1915 almost 200 battalions had been authorized for the C.E.F. in addition to the innumerable supporting and ancillary units that made up a modern army. Eventually the total would reach 270.

Like most crusades, the recruiting drive was costly, wasteful, frustrating, and an ultimate failure. It depended on a confidence trick: that units raised by respected community leaders and composed of friends and neighbours would see action together. By August 1916, the Canadian Corps was complete with forty-eight battalions. Thereafter, except for a few replacements, the composition was unaltered. The units recruited in Canada reached England only to be broken up. The junior officers and men went to France to fill gaps in the Corps; senior officers were left in frustrated idleness.[52]

In English-speaking Canada recruiting was a crusade betrayed. In Quebec there was no crusade. Support for the war was an obligation dutifully accepted by the higher clergy and the more obedient Party newspapers. Apart from Dr. Arthur Mignault, wealthy French Canadians showed little inclination to become Sam Hughes's colonels. The

---

[50] Joseph Levitt, introduction to Elizabeth Armstrong, *The Crisis of Quebec* (rev. ed.; Toronto, 1974), pp. xii-xiii.

[51] See Ken Adachi, *The Enemy That Never Was: A History of the Japanese Canadians* (Toronto, 1976), pp. 101-103; Robin Winks, *The Blacks in Canada* (New Haven and Montreal, 1971), pp. 313-19.

[52] For the reaction of one victim, see Leslie M. Frost, *Fighting Men* (Toronto, 1967).

desperate shortage of competent French Canadian officers was almost immediately apparent.

Later, Colonel Mignault claimed that the press of volunteers forced Ottawa to authorize a 41st and a 57th Battalion for Quebec. Winter and unemployment played as important a part as patriotism.[53] Soldiers were recruited, claimed the scornful *nationalistes*, "des chômeurs, des assistés du refuge Meurling, voire des 'toughs'—des gibiers de prison à qui l'on offrait cette voie de rehabilitation."[54] The 22nd Battalion seemed to exhaust the available officer talent. To command the 41st Battalion, Hughes chose a former cadet instructor whose ineptitude eventually proved fatal to the unit. The second-in-command, an undischarged bankrupt, absconded with $900 of the regimental funds. His successor was a drunkard. So was the chaplain. To complete the battalion and get it to England, the authorities finally added a company of Russians recruited in western Canada.[55] In England the assistant adjutant was convicted of murder. His death sentence was commuted on the petition that he was notoriously feeble-minded.[56] While the 41st Battalion soon dissolved into reinforcements, its appalling reputation damaged recruiting in Quebec, and French Canadian standing in the C.E.F.[57]

To find other colonels Hughes turned to the militia and to the few French Canadian officers in the 1st Division. The 69th Battalion was recruited by Lieutenant-Colonel Adolphe Dansereau, son of a founder of *La Presse*, a veteran of Ypres and the youngest colonel in the C.E.F. Captain Hercule Barré of the 14th Battalion was brought home to raise the 150th Battalion. In October 1915, Hughes invited Armand Lavergne, whom he admired as an equally furious controversialist, to recruit a unit. Lavergne publicly refused but to the general astonishment, the invitation was taken up by an even more ardent battler in the nationalist cause, Olivar Asselin. His reasons were complex. Notably anti-clerical, he insisted that he would embarrass the bishops by obeying their pastoral advice to enlist. The truth, according to his biographer, was that Asselin loved France and ached to see action. His penalty was to be denounced as an apostate by the nationalist press and to be pursued with rumours that he had enlisted to escape a court judgment.[58]

---

[53] Mignault to Borden, July 7, 1917, Kemp Papers, vol. 63, p. 4.

[54] Rumilly, *Québec*, vol. 20, p. 75.

[55] Desmond Morton, "The Short, Unhappy Life of the 41st Battalion, C.E.F.," *Queen's Quarterly*, vol. 81, no. 1 (Spring, 1974); R.G. 9, Carson File, 8-15-17.

[56] Court of Criminal Appeal, *R. v. Georges Codere*, February 28, 1916, p. 6, cited in P.A.C., R.G. 13, file 502-30.

[57] For example, Ward, *A Party Politician*, p. 46.

[58] Marcel Gagnon, *La vie orageuse d'Olivar Asselin* (Montreal, 1962), pp. 174-75; Rumilly, *Québec*, vol. 20, p. 123; vol. 21, pp. 28-29.

Unlike others, Asselin modestly accepted the rank of major and another young officer from the 14th, Henri DesRosiers, was brought back to Canada to command the new 163rd Battalion. Asselin insisted that his *Poils aux Pattes* must be an elite unit and his prestige undoubtedly drew more impressive young officers than did rival battalions. Among them were Gustave Lanctôt and Henri Le Royer, a future air ace. Asselin's energy and popularity also drew recruits and he relentlessly prosecuted those who deserted.

Rival units had no such standards of discipline. To Asselin's indignation, a Conservative lawyer and former commanding officer of the 85th Regiment, Tancrède Pagnuelo, had also been authorized to recruit in Montreal for his 206th Battalion. While Asselin promised his men glory and sacrifice, Pagnuelo's agents emphasized warm uniforms, regular pay, and the promise of being "le dernier régiment à partir, le premier à profiter de la victoire." In Asselin's view, Pagnuelo's unit could only be a conspiracy to discredit French Canadians.[59] The angry ex-journalist demanded to see Hughes and insisted that his fledgling battalion must be transferred at once. Hughes obliged by sending it to do garrison duty in Bermuda.

In further revenge, men of the 206th Battalion were transferred to fill up the strength of the 163rd. It was, insisted local staff officers, the neatest solution to a very embarrassing problem. Just how embarrassing soon became apparent. Beside himself with rage, the unhappy Pagnuelo paraded his men and virtually counselled them to desert. The ensuing investigation revealed much more. With the connivance of his officers, Pagnuelo had devised a system of fining his men and pocketing the money. His quartermaster and close confederate, Major Theo Grothé, was accused of arresting the canteen contractors, seizing their stock without so much as an inventory, and running the canteen for his own profit. He had also enlisted his fourteen-year-old son as a sergeant and collected his pay.[60] When Pagnuelo was cashiered and sentenced to six months imprisonment, it was for perjury and fraud as much as for his highly-publicized outburst.[61]

By the summer of 1916 the skeletons of six battalions recruiting in Quebec were gathered at Valcartier. As military units they were undisciplined, weak in numbers, and plagued by bad officers and desertion. For many in French Canada this agglomeration of military ineffectives represented a last hope of forming a distinct French Canadian brigade in the Canadian Corps. In a letter to Borden, Gustave Lanctôt

---

[59] Gagnon, *Asselin*, pp. 180-81.

[60] On the 206th Battalion, see R.G. 24, vol. 1564, HQ 683-263, files 1-5, especially Captain G. Barclay to Brig. Gen. E. W. Wilson, July 30, 1916; ibid., file 5. (Lavergne acted as lawyer for the aggrieved contractors.)

[61] *Canadian Annual Review* (1916), p. 353; Montreal *Star*, December 5-8, 1916; P.C. 3102, December 14, 1916.

blended military and political arguments. Such a brigade would satisfy
the ambition of French Canadian officers and convince men in the
ranks that they would be properly understood. "It will thus satisfy the
province at large, civilians and military men, with the result of increasing the goodwill in all spheres and of disposing better the people for the
party in power."[62]

The project was hopeless. Even the officers at Valcartier saw its
futility. When the 206th Battalion dissolved after Pagnuelo's speech,
there was an uncontrolled scramble for its arms, equipment, and
stores. Although suspicion pointed to Lieutenant-Colonel Onésime
Readman's 167th Battalion, no staff officer even attempted to recover
the losses. In due course, when Readman's own battalion was dissolved,
he and several of his officers went on trial for fraud and forgery.[63]
Perhaps there are no bad troops but there certainly were bad officers in
some of the French Canadian battalions.

Scandal was by no means reserved to French-speaking units.
Comparable disintegration, lack of discipline, and corruption could be
found in English-speaking battalions. English Canadian officers were
also court-martialled and cashiered though their conduct never gained
the notoriety of Tancrède Pagnuelo in both the French and English
press. Nor did all French Canadian battalions share the reputation of
the 41st, the 167th, and the 206th. The 189th Battalion, recruited by
Lieutenant-Colonel P. A. Piuze from the hardbitten farmers and
fishermen of the Lower St. Lawrence, was universally recognized as an
efficient, well-disciplined unit. Two of its members, Lieutenant Jean
Brillant and Corporal Joseph Keable, later won the Victoria Cross in
the ranks of the 22nd Battalion. Of all Quebeckers, Piuze's men were
most remote from both the arguments of Henri Bourassa and the
attraction of well-paid jobs in Quebec's booming munitions industry.[64]

By the summer of 1916 there were few such regions left in the
province. Even the issue of Franco-Ontarian schools was no longer
used to oppose enlistment. The limited number of French Canadians
willing to volunteer "for a somewhat interesting adventure in a foreign
country" had long since been reached. The remainder were prodded
to fury by sneers from recruiting sergeants and Ontario newspapers.[65]

On September 15-18, 1916, the 22nd Battalion lost one-third of its
men in capturing Courcelette. Two weeks later another one-third fell

[62] Lanctôt to Borden, March 17, 1916; Borden Papers, OC 209, p. 21286 and see
also memorandum, pp. 21286-88. See also Mignault to Borden, November 13, 1916,
ibid., p. 21293.

[63] Major Gregor Barclay to Adjutant General, January 25, 1918, R.G. 24, HQ
683-263-2. See also HQ 683-263-7.

[64] Brigadier General A. O. Fages to Militia Council, August 26, 1916, R.G. 24, vol.
4515, SD 17-12-1.

[65] Rumilly, *Québec*, vol. 21, pp. 69, 158.

in the hopeless struggle for Regina Trench. To fill the gaps, drafts from Valcartier were badly needed. In November the 163rd sailed from Bermuda to England. Within a month, over Asselin's protests, the battalion was broken up to provide reinforcements.[66]

By then Hughes was no longer Minister of Militia. His successor, Sir Edward Kemp, did what might have been done much earlier. Colonel Arthur Mignault was summoned from the French Canadian hospital at St. Cloud and appointed chairman of a French-Canadian recruiting committee. Even for a man of his optimism, the task was impossible. Breaking its own rule, the Militia Department advanced funds for advertising. Mignault over-spent his allocation threefold, appointed recruiting officers, and despatched them across the province. By the end of March, Mignault's committee had found less than 500 men, many of whom were rejected for medical reasons.[67]

In the spring of 1917 the government tried again. P.-E. Blondin, one of Borden's last remaining French Canadian ministers, became a colonel and set out with the militia's most senior French Canadian, Major-General Francois Lessard, on a last attempt to recruit a battalion. Mignault's recruiting officers found themselves part of a 258th Battalion. Blondin was physically assaulted. Meetings disrupted. By mid-June, Blondin could count only ninety-two recruits, some of them remnants of earlier battalions.[68]

How did French Canadian officers overseas regard the humiliation which the war imposed on their province? The records, official and private, are almost wholly silent.[69] Perhaps, as Rumilly suggests, they were too remote from Quebec, too preoccupied by the war, too much engaged by military propaganda to have more sympathy for Bourassa than for their fellow sufferers. Perhaps, like other soldiers, they had come to despise politics. Olivar Asselin, guarding his rank of major but serving as a platoon commander in the 22nd, mixed courage and self-sacrifice with an unresisted temptation to lecture his superiors on their duties. Understandably, Colonel Tremblay got rid of him at his earliest opportunity. When Asselin eventually returned to the front, it was in an English-speaking unit.[70]

To the very end there would be only one French-speaking battalion in the Canadian Corps. After conscription was imposed, pressure revived for the formation of a French Canadian Brigade. This time, it

---

[66] Gagnon, *Asselin*, p. 185.

[67] On the Mignault Committee, R.G. 24, vol. 2552, HQ 1982-1-91; P.C. 3050/December 11, 1916. On the results, J. W. Borden to Sir Eugene Fiset, March 20, 1917, ibid.; Granatstein and Hitsman, *Broken Promises*, p. 33.

[68] On Blondin, see ibid.; Rumilly, *Québec*, vol. 22, pp. 49-50 and passim.

[69] The work of J.-P. Gagnon on the composition of the 22nd Battalion will add greatly to our knowledge of this unit although his study has focussed on men in the ranks.

[70] Gagnon, *Asselin*, pp. 187-88. See also Lapointe, *Soldier of Quebec*, pp. 30-31.

had full backing from Sir Robert Borden, desperate to do anything to pacify an outraged Quebec.[71] In England the argument was joined by Hercule Barré, whose 150th Battalion had formed part of the short-lived 5th Canadian Division, and by Henri DesRosiers, commanding the French Canadian reinforcement battalion.

The decision of the Corps commander, Sir Arthur Currie, was chilling and final. After consulting his division and brigade commanders, he reported that they did not want so much as a company of French Canadians. The experience of the 14th Battalion had apparently been too unsatisfactory. "My own opinion is that they should not be kept separate," Currie concluded, "they are Canadians the same as everybody else, and the sooner it is so regarded the better it will be for the national life of our country."[72]

If the war had lasted longer, changes would have come. The compromise, eventually accepted by Currie, was that French Canadian reinforcements would be sent to the seven battalions originally recruited from Quebec. By the time of the Armistice their transformation was well underway.[73]

It was not reflected by a conversion to French-speaking officers. Like the rest of the Corps, the 22nd Battalion had turned increasingly to its own ranks to find replacements for its heavy officer casualties. The era of subalterns, fresh from school and a few weeks of drill, was over. Even promotion from the ranks was insufficient. After the deadly battle of Cherisy, even Colonel DesRosiers found his chance to command the 22nd Battalion in the field. It was at Wasmes, not far from Mons, on November 11, that the war ended for French Canadians. By then the only senior French Canadian officers in the Corps were Brigadier-Generals H. A. Panet and Thomas Tremblay.

In the aftermath of the war, Canadian officers struggled to learn its lessons. They did so in a country that wished for nothing so fervently as to forget about the war. Henri Bourassa, who had been execrated as an agent of the Kaiser, saw his view of Canadian national interest prevail even as he retreated in his own disillusionment to a new and more narrow loyalty. The cure for imperial-nationalism was the price—60,000 dead and almost as many more torn and mutilated in mind and body. Henceforth, in world affairs, Canadians would consult their own interests as Bourassa had warned. If they did, there would be no more crusades in Europe.

---

[71] Borden to Kemp, April 29, 1918, Borden Papers, OC 209, p. 21305.

[72] Currie to Turner, March 14, 1918, P.A.C., Turner Papers, p. 5756.

[73] Turner to Currie, March 26, 1918, ibid., p. 5755; Kemp to Borden, May 7, 1918, Borden Papers, OC 209, 21313.

That could not, of course, be the conviction of most of the officers assembled in that postwar novelty: National Defence Headquarters. In the postwar reorganization, a reluctant cabinet finally surrendered to the repeated insistence of its military advisors. French Canada would have its own unit in the permanent force, the Royal 22ᵉ Regiment.[74] With that reform and its limited consequences, the most critical issue in Canadian defence was left until, indeed, there was another crusade in Europe. Once again, a conflict of loyalties would arise.

---

[74] On the Royal 22ᵉ Régiment, see J. A. Swettenham, *McNaughton*, vol. 1: *1887-1939* (Toronto, 1968), pp. 186-87.

BECK, ROMMEL AND THE NAZIS: THE DILEMMA OF THE GERMAN ARMY

PETER HOFFMANN

1

IN THE first decade after World War II, received historiography held that soldiers of the German armed forces, particularly high-ranking officers who had resisted or plotted against Hitler, were patriotic heroes, and martyrs if they suffered death as a result.[1] There was always a historiographic subculture supported by unrepentant former functionaries and friends of the Nazi regime; it sought to deny, or to balance with Allied excesses, the regime's crimes, and to discredit as traitors those who fought against the Nazi regime. This subculture still exists, and its production of printed material is growing.[2] Another phenomenon, however, makes it appear less and less shrill, less distinguishable from well-founded, mainstream historiography: it has been the tendency, during the last fifteen years, to emphasize social-forces and class-orientation theories of historical explanation, which tend to blur the line between apologetic writers and those who are motivated to attack the world of their parents, who seek to identify with an ideology other than Christianity, Capitalism, and Nationalism.[3] The effect is a

---

[1] Hans Rothfels, *The German Opposition to Hitler* (London: Oswald Wolff, 1961); Gerhard Ritter, *The German Resistance: Carl Goerdeler's Struggle against Tyranny* (London: Allen and Unwin, 1958); Eberhard Zeller, *The Flame of Freedom: The German Struggle against Hitler* (London: Oswald Wolff, 1967).

[2] [Hans W. Hagen], *Zwischen Eid und Befehl (Revolte um Hitler)* (Vienna: Verlag Karl Kühne, 1951); Hans W. Hagen, *Zwischen Eid und Befehl: Tatzeugenbericht von den Ereignissen am 20. Juli 1944 in Berlin und "Wolfsschanze,"* 4th ed. (Munich: Türmer Verlag 1968); [Otto Ernst] Remer, *20. Juli 1944* (Hamburg-Neuhaus/Oste: Verlag Hans Siep, 1951); Annelies von Ribbentrop, *Die Kriegsschuld des Widerstandes: Aus britischen Geheimdokumenten 1938/39* (Leoni am Starnberger See: Druffel-Verlag, 1974); Karl Balzer, *Der 20. Juli und der Landesverrat: Dokumentation über Verratshandlungen im deutschen Widerstand* (Pro. Oldendorf: Verlag K. W. Schütz K.G., 1971); *Verrat und Widerstand im Dritten Reich: Referate und Arbeitsergebnisse des zeitgeschichtlichen Kongresses der Gesellschaft für Freie Publizistik vom 26.-28. Mai 1978 in Kassel* (Coburg: Nation Europa Verlag, 1978); David Irving, *Hitler's War* (London: Hodder and Stoughton, [1977]).

[3] Hans Mommsen, "Nationalsozialismus oder Hitlerismus?," in Michael Bosch (ed.), *Persönlichkeit und Struktur in der Geschichte* (Düsseldorf: Pädagogischer Verlag Schwann, 1977), pp. 62-71; Andreas Hillgruber, "Tendenzen, Ergebnisse und Perspektiven der gegenwärtigen Hitler-Forschung," *Historische Zeitschrift*, vol. 226 (1978), pp. 600-602.

de-emphasis of the individual personality and its role in history, a de-emphasis of the ethical basis of individuals' actions.

One of the main themes of the "revisionist" school runs: the alleged resisters in the armed forces all agreed with Hitler's aims; they were only a little critical of his methods. But when they saw that he was unsuccessful and when his imminent downfall threatened their own privileges and powers, their thoughts turned to treason, and to how they might salvage their vested interests by dumping Hitler. In the past few years, Colonel-General Ludwig Beck has been portrayed along such or similar lines by Klaus-Jürgen Müller and by Nicholas Reynolds; Heinz Höhne made an effort to dismantle the reputation of Admiral Wilhelm Canaris as an opponent of Hitler; Christian Müller, a Swiss writer, and Kurt Finker, an East German historian, both emphasize that Colonel Claus Graf Schenk von Stauffenberg did not actively fight Hitler until very late in the war; Field Marshal Erwin Rommel and Lieutenant-General Hans Speidel were denied their roles as opponents of Hitler by David Irving.[4]

Issues of oath and treason were always on a high level of consciousness in German military thought. A violation of the oath of allegiance is considered treasonous, and overtones of loyalty, rooted in the mediaeval feudal system, are strongly associated with the oath, giving it an emotional dimension. The romantic and neo-romantic currents in German intellectual history through the nineteenth and into the twentieth centuries, coupled with a widespread rejection of utilitarian, pluralistic viewpoints, and the tradition of the monarch and "leader" as actual and effective supreme commander of military forces, may have perpetuated such pre-modern attitudes in the German context more than elsewhere.

German law distinguishes between treason against the government (*Hochverrat*) and treason against the country (*Landesverrat*).[5] The first refers to illegal subversion and activities aiming at the overthrow of government through illegal means (*coup d'état*, rebellion). The sec-

---

[4] Klaus-Jürgen Müller, *Das Heer und Hitler: Armee und nationalsozialistisches Regime 1933-1940* (Stuttgart: Deutsche Verlags-Anstalt, 1969); Klaus-Jürgen Müller, "Staat und Politik im Denken Ludwig Becks," *Historische Zeitschrift*, vol. 215 (1972), pp. 607-31; Nicholas Reynolds, *Treason Was No Crime: Ludwig Beck. Chief of the German General Staff* (London: William Kimber, 1976); Heinz Höhne, *Canaris: Patriot im Zwielicht* (Munich: C. Bertelsmann Verlag, [1976]); Christian Müller, *Oberst i. G. Stauffenberg* (Düsseldorf: Drost Verlag, [1970]); Kurt Finker, *Stauffenberg und der 20. Juli 1944* (Berlin: Union Verlag, 1967; 4th ed., 1973); David Irving, *The Trail of the Fox* (New York: E. P. Dutton, [1977]). N.B.: Ranks given in the text and notes are *linguistic* translations of the German ranks, therefore not necessarily their equivalents in the British or American ranking systems. Thus a German *Wehrmacht Generalmajor* is translated Major-General, but the rank corresponds to Brigadier.

[5] E. Kohlrausch (ed.), *Strafgesetzbuch für das Deutsche Reich mit Nebengesetzen* (Berlin and Leipzig: Walter de Gruyter, 1930), §§87-91.

ond concept deals with damage to the integrity of the nation's territory and population, with serious violations of her interests, and especially with actual and potential damage to the military might of the country. The legal position was tightly defined and the penalties were heavy, but the German Supreme Court (*Reichsgericht*) in the 1920s recognized that the realities of life cannot always be prescribed in codes, and that laws require interpretation if they are to be meaningful and applicable. When the first President of the German Republic after World War I, Friedrich Ebert, was accused after his death in 1925 of having committed treason because he had assumed the leadership of a strike of munitions workers in 1917, his accuser was sued successfully. Since Ebert had acted to contain and end the strike, the German Supreme Court decided on October 20, 1931 that it was not a case of treason against the country if an action that would otherwise fall under the law of treason was engaged in with the intention of averting much greater damage.[6] In the National-Socialist state, scores upon scores of new laws were made, and old ones were changed to suit the whims and arbitrary government of Hitler and his henchmen.[7] The coverage of the law of treason was vastly expanded and the penalties made extremely severe. Constitutional principles, whether formally suspended or not, were constantly and blatantly violated. But, as before 1933, two fundamental decisions were necessary for anyone contemplating what was formally regarded as treason: whether the "treason" would be useful or even required for the welfare of the country and the nation, and whether the law prohibiting it was right and just in the circumstances. The 1931 decision of the Supreme Court certainly applied to the actions of Lieutenant-Colonel Hans Oster, of Colonel-General Beck, of Admiral Canaris, of Field Marshal Rommel, and of Field Marshal von Witzleben, although this interpretation was not valid in a state in which Hitler was the self-appointed "supreme judge" (*Oberster Gerichtsherr*) whose actions (as in the Röhm Massacre) were to be regarded as *eo ipso* legal.

Beck at least was familiar with considerations of what constituted treason: two officers in a regiment he commanded in 1930 were accused of treason against the government. Beck was not only a witness at the trial but was also very much concerned over the fate of the two young officers under his command.[8] One might, however, refer to a much older tradition of just opposition and resistance to authority which is entirely inseparable from the tradition of oath and loyalty. The

---

[6] *Entscheidungen des Reichsgerichts in Strafsachen*, vol. 65 (Berlin and Leipzig: Walter de Gruyter, 1931), pp. 422-33.

[7] Ilse Staff (ed.), *Justiz im Dritten Reich: Eine Dokumentation* (Frankfurt/M.: Fischer Taschenbuch Verlag, 1964; 2nd ed., 1978), passim.

[8] Peter Bucher, *Der Reichswehrprozess: Der Hochverrat der Ulmer Reichswehroffiziere 1929/30* (Boppard am Rhein: Harald Boldt Verlag, [1967]).

concept of the *rex iustus* and *rex iniustus* was familiar to mediaeval feudal society. Breach of fealty could be committed by the king as well as by his vassal, and obligations were valid only on the basis of mutual loyalty.[9] Both the Reformation and the developing popular sovereignty theories depended, explicitly or implicitly, on the assumption of a right to resist authority. Theodor Beza, a Calvinist, wrote that the right to resist unjust authorities belonged not simply to anyone, but to the authority immediately subordinated to the one acting unjustly— if there was no superior authority that could provide a remedy. But if the appropriate authorities failed in their proper functions, if they failed to advise the prince to govern justly, and if they failed to oppose and resist injustice, the right to resist devolved, according to Beza, upon lower authorities, and, if they also failed, finally upon the citizen.[10] Obviously such fundamental positions cannot be taught generally; no compendium can be provided to make recognizable for everyone those situations in which he must resist authority. Both the situation and the individual acting in it will always tend to be exceptional. Conditions preventing or seeking to hinder the proper exercise of responsibilities—such as those of the military commander who is bound by ethics of warfare and by the responsibility for his men and for his country—may thus turn what would be treasonable mutiny in ordinary conditions into the due exercise of responsible authority. If no laws, statutes, or clear precedents can be referred to, the conscience must take their place. The basis of action is then the fundamental regard for human life and for justice, which needs no written laws to be valid and effective.

Beck and Rommel are representative, each in a particular respect, of the many who answered the challenge of such extreme existential situations. Beck, an intellectual soldier and strategic thinker, reached a position of resistance well before the outbreak of war. Rommel, a combat soldier and supremely gifted tactician of offence, arrived at similar conclusions late in the war. The basic consideration which both fell back on was the same: human life.

2

LUDWIG BECK was born in Biebrich on the Rhine in 1880. He died on the evening of July 20, 1944, after the attempt to overthrow Hitler,

---

[9] Karl Kroeschell, *Deutsche Rechtsgeschichte 2* (Reinbek bei Hamburg: Rowohlt Taschenbuch Verlag, 1973), pp. 184, 224-30.

[10] Ioannes Althusius, *Politica methodice digesta atque exemplis sacris et profanis illustrata, cui in fine adiuncta est Oratio panegyrica de necessitate, utilitate et antiquitate scholarum* (Herbornae, 1603); Théodore Bèze, *Du droit des magistrats* (Geneva: Droz, 1970; first published, 1574).

in which he had participated, had failed. In 1898 Beck joined No. 15 Prussian Field Artillery Regiment in Strassburg. He attended the War Academy in Berlin from 1908 to 1911, joined the Great General Staff in 1912, served in it through World War I, and held troop-command and staff positions after the war. From October 1929 to September 1931 Beck commanded No. 5 Artillery Regiment in Fulda, Ludwigs-burg, and Ulm, and from October 1, 1932 to September 30, 1933 he commanded the 1st Cavalry Division in Frankfurt on Oder. From October 1, 1933 he was Chief of the Troop Office (*Chef des Truppen-namtes*) in the *Reichswehr* Ministry; this office was renamed Chief of the General Staff of the Army (*Chef des Generalstabes des Heeres*) from July 1, 1935. Beck held the position until he turned it over to General Halder on August 27, 1938.[11] During those years, the Commander-in-Chief of the Army (*Chef der Herresleitung*, later *Oberbefehlshaber des Heeres*) was Colonel-General Werner Freiherr von Fritsch, as successor to Colonel-General Kurt Freiherr von Hammerstein-Equord, from February 1, 1934 to February 4, 1938.[12]

It must be understood that Hitler's appointment as Chancellor on January 30, 1933, by the venerated Field Marshal and *Reich* President, Paul von Hindenburg, was not regarded by most of those whose politi-cal preference lay somewhere to the right of Communists and Socialists, as a *coup d'état*, as an illegal takeover by a gang of political hoodlums. Although the new government immediately proceeded to violate and suspend the essential provisions of the Constitution of the Republic, establishing step by step a one-party dictatorship, Hitler's accession had, at least in form, been legal. Creeping dictatorship had been a feature of the Hindenburg-Brüning, Hindenburg-Papen, and Hindenburg-Schleicher emergency regimes, and its continuation could appear justified by a continuing economic and political crisis. The threat of communism and of Marxist conspiracies against German national values, against private property, and against the social order was put to effective use by the propaganda of the National-Socialists.[13] Finally, military men regarded their establishment as aloof from "party politics," and as sacrosanct. There seemed to be no reason to confront and oppose the new government, unless the role of the armed forces as such—that is to most intents and purposes the army—was threatened, as by the attempts of the *Sturmabteilung* (S.A.) to join and to become and

---

[11] Wolfgang Foerster, *Generaloberst Ludwig Beck: Sein Kampf gegen den Krieg* (Munich: Isar Verlag, 1953), pp. 9-29; Friedrich Hossbach, *Swischen Wehrmacht und Hitler 1934-1938*, 2nd ed. (Göttingen: Vandenhoeck & Ruprecht, 1965), passim; Wolf Keilig, *Das deutsche Heer 1939-1945: Gliederung-Einsatz-Stellenbesetzung* (Bad Nauheim: Verlag Hans-Henning Podzun, 1956 et seq.), 211/18.

[12] Ibid., 211/91.

[13] Peter Hoffmann, *The History of the German Resistance 1933-1945* (Cambridge, Mass.: M.I.T. Press, 1977), pp. 3-35.

revolutionize the army of the National-Socialist state—whereupon the army leadership supported the elimination of the S.A.'s leadership.[14] The method—mass murder without any appearance of a judicial process—became apparent only after the support had been given.

The increased apprehension and reserve that many felt toward the regime was, as one would expect in any state so dissimilar to certain South American republics, still a long way from open or clandestine rebellion. Economic recovery, foreign policy successes which gradually dismantled the restrictions of the deeply resented Treaty of Versailles, spectaculars such as the Olympic Games of 1936 in Berlin, and general international recognition in many forms rather moderated the mood of those who had begun thinking of ways to rid Germany of its National-Socialist government. This was, to be sure, balanced in the minds of many by the regime's oppressive policies, by persecutions, and especially by the pogrom of November 1938. But it was finally the threat of war that tipped the scales against Hitler, though, again, only relatively few individuals, as in all comparable societies, took steps to bring about an illegal overthrow of the government. At the same time, and certainly up to the point when war might endanger all that had been achieved, it was natural for military men to support a policy of rearmament proportionate to the state of military preparedness of Germany's neighbours and other powers. It seemed reasonable that Germany, in the face of the strength of the French army, should have an army larger than a mere 100,000. And it also seemed reasonable that she should have tanks, an air force, and a stronger navy, surrounded as she was by French-sponsored alliances (France-Poland, 1921; France-Poland-Czechoslovakia, 1925; Yugoslavia-Czechoslovakia-Roumania, 1921-1933; U.S.S.R.-Czechoslovakia, 1935; U.S.S.R.-France, 1935).

Beck's support for a measure of rearmament is then not a contradiction to his increasingly critical attitude towards the regime—an attitude that culminated, in 1938, in Beck's attempts to bring about a *coup d'état* if Hitler could not be persuaded to give up his war policy. Soon after the war, a historian who knew Beck very well and who had access to his papers, portrayed Beck as a man who always opposed the aggressive elements of Hitler's foreign policy.[15] More recently a historian who is also fully familiar with Beck's papers has argued that the origins of Beck's opposition to the National-Socialist regime were not to be found in a fundamental rejection of policies of violence and faithlessness, but in Hitler's failure to accept Beck's view that the Chief of the General Staff of the army must have a regular advisory function with the Chief of State in all essential policy decisions including, and

[14] Müller, *Das Heer und Hitler*, pp. 88-141.
[15] Foerster, *Generaloberst Ludwig Beck*, passim.

especially, foreign policy decisions.[16] There is a good deal of evidence for both lines of argument. It is thus a question of how conclusive the evidence is in either case, and of which of Beck's objections was more fundamental in terms of motivation as well as in terms of the consequences Beck was willing to face in adhering to his convictions.

The Prussian and, after reorganization of the armies of the German states and after the foundation of the *Reich* in 1871, the German Chief of the General Staff of the army had a position at the level of cabinet rank. He was privileged to report directly to the Supreme Commander of the armed forces, the King and Emperor, being equal in this respect to the War Minister.[17] The influence of the Chief of the General Staff of the army decreased relatively under the regime of Emperor William II, in part through the Emperor's efforts to exert more personal control over the armed forces and over foreign policy, and also through his practice of permitting a number of other military functionaries to report directly to him. These included, besides the Prussian War Minister, the Chief of the Admiral Staff, Admiral von Pohl, the State Secretary of the *Reichs Marine Amt*, Admiral von Tirpitz; the Chief of the Emperor's Naval Cabinet (*Marine Kabinett*), Admiral von Müller; the Commander of the Fleet, Admiral Ingenohl; the Chiefs of the Emperor's Military Cabinet, Generals von Albedyll and von Lyncker; and military attachés in foreign capitals. During World War I, through the preponderance of the land forces and the weakness of both the political leadership (the Chancellor) and the Supreme Commander (the Emperor), the power of the Chief of the General Staff was greatly expanded; but the power of his First Deputy, the Quartermaster General, became even greater in the Third Supreme Army Command (*3. Oberste Herresleitung*), mainly because of the personalities of Hindenburg and Ludendorff, the chief of the General Staff and the Quartermaster General respectively. Their political power was sufficient to effect, among other things, the replacement of the Chancellor, Bethmann Hollweg, in 1917, and the transfer of Lenin and other revolutionaries from Switzerland to Russia in the same year.[18] In the 1920s, after the Treaty of Versailles, the position of the Chief of the General Staff was scaled down in importance and power by the virtual disarmament of Germany, by partial Allied military occupation, by the

[16] Müller, "Staat und Politik," passim.

[17] Graf Helmuth von Moltke, *Geschichte des deutsch-französischen Krieges von 1870-71 nebst einem Aufsatz "über den angeblichen Kriegsrath in den Kriegen König Wilhelms I.,"* 2nd ed. (Berlin: Ernst Siegfried Mittler und Sohn, 1891); Michael Balfour, *The Kaiser and His Times* (New York: W. W. Norton, 1972), pp. 90-91; Gordon A. Craig, *The Politics of the Prussian Army 1640-1945* (New York: Oxford University Press, 1964), pp. 217-54, 225.

[18] *Handbuch der Deutschen Geschichte*, founded by Otto Brandt, continued by Arnold Oskarf Mayer, and newly edited by Leo Just, vol. 4, part 1 (Frankfurt am Main: Akademische Verlagsgesellschaft Athenaion), 2nd section, pp. 37-53, 56.

limitations placed upon German foreign policy, and by a changed hierarchy of command. The Chief of the General Staff of the army now advised and assisted an army general who was Commander-in-Chief of the army (*Chef der Heeresleitung*), and who reported to a War Minister (to May 21, 1935, *Reichswehr* Minister, or Armed Forces Minister). Only the War Minister himself had cabinet rank. Presumably he would lead the armed forces in time of war; but the Minister in Hitler's cabinet, Field Marshal von Blomberg, was not considered capable of this task. The head of state, the President of the Republic, was titular Supreme Commander of the armed forces. The fact that this was, from 1925 to August 2, 1934, Field Marshal von Hindenburg, again made actual power and control more diffuse. Hitler gradually, step by step, moved to concentrate the powers of control in his own hands: upon Hindenburg's death, he assumed the presidency; he frequently made decisions affecting the armed forces; he abolished the War Ministry in January-February 1938, replacing Blomberg by an office chief (General Keitel as Chief of O.K.W. [*Oberkommando der Wehrmacht*]), and replacing Fritsch by Brauchitsch, who promised to associate the army more closely with the state and party leadership; finally, in December 1941, he assumed personal command of the army dismissing Brauchitsch without replacing him.[19]

In a memorandum dated January 15, 1934, Beck demanded for the highest-ranking military person co-responsible participation in decisions with any reference to war, that is, in all foreign policy matters of any significance.[20] Hitler would not tolerate such a role played by Blomberg or Fritsch, but neither of them really claimed it. When Beck refers to this role, he claims it for the *Feldherr*, or war leader, leaving open whether this would be the War Minister, the Commander-in-Chief of the Army, the Chief of the Troop Office, or the Chief of the General Staff of the army. Although Beck himself is vague on this point, Klaus-Jürgen Müller maintains that it was the denial of this role to *Beck* that was the source of his opposition to Hitler and to the National-Socialist regime.[21] He cites a letter by Beck dated November 28, 1918 in which Beck dealt with the institutional and personal inability of William II to lead effectively in political and military affairs,

[19] Müller, *Das Heer und Hitler*, p. 627; *Die deutsche Reishcverfassung vom 11. August 1919* ([Berlin:] Reichszentrale für Heimatdienst, 1919), art. 46-48; *Handbuch der Deutschen Geschichte*, pp. 117-20; M. Schreiber (ed.), *Heeresverwaltungs-Taschenbuch: Hand- und Nachschlagebuch über Verwaltungsangelegenheiten für den deutschen Soldaten und Heeres- beamten 1937/38* (Grimmen in Pommern: Verlag Alfred Waberg, [1937]), pp. 26-27, 35-38; Reynolds, *Treason Was No Crime*, pp. 109-10; Hoffmann, *History*, pp. 36-46.

[20] Müller, *Das Heer und Hitler*, pp. 627-33; Müller, "Staat und Politik," pp. 614-15, 626-28.

[21] Müller, "Staat und Politik," pp. 610, 626-28; Müller, *Das Heer und Hitler*, p. 590.

thus relinquishing leadership in both to Hindenburg and Ludendorff. Beck thought that a "responsible ministry," a cabinet, should have been the political partner of the military leaders on an equal level, with the Emperor above them as representative and bearer of the Crown and the highest authority and source of power in the state. Thus Beck did not discuss, as Müller believes, a "disturbed relationship" between political and military leadership, but rather the absence of any political authority on the same level with military authority. The memorandum of January 15, 1934 is concerned with the organization of an Armed Forces Ministry headed by an immediate Supreme Commander of the Armed Forces in peace and war, thus ensuring continuity. This Minister and Supreme Commander had to be capable of exercising supreme command: he could not be Blomberg, Hitler's War Minister. The charts Beck prepared clearly show what he was interested in, and it was the same concern that he had expressed in his letter of November 28, 1918: a proper balance of political and military considerations in decisions affecting the state and the nation.[22]

Beck's memorandum was written eight months before Hindenburg's death and Hitler's usurpation of the powers of the President of the Republic; by that time, the imbalance had become even greater than it had been in view "of the person of the present Armed Forces Minister [Blomberg]."[23] By February 4, 1938, the armed forces were increasingly controlled by the head of state himself, and his combined political and military authority was not balanced by military leaders capable of fulfilling their duty of advising and, if need be, restraining the political leadership. When a policy was pursued, as before 1914 and again since 1933 (as Hitler had made abundantly clear to military leaders),[24] which could or must involve the German army in conflict with other armies, the strength of those armies, their political and economic resources, their allies, etc., had to be considered in assessing their military potential vis-à-vis the German army, in large part at least on the basis of information gathered regularly by the Fourth Quartermaster Division (*Oberquartiermeister IV/Fremde Heere Ost, Fremde Heere West*, and *Attaché Gruppe*) and through the Armed Forces Intelligence Office (*Amtsgruppe Auslandnachrichten und Abwehr, Ausl./Abwehr* for short, in the *Wehrmachtamt*, from 1938 in *O.K.W.*). *Now* it was clearly necessary, in view of the failings of Brauchitsch, and in view of the abolition of the War Ministry, that the Chief of the General Staff of the army have access to the head of state.

---

[22] Müller, *Das Heer und Hitler*, pp. 630-33.
[23] Ibid., p. 627.
[24] Thilo Vogelsang, "Neue Dokumente zur Geschichte der Reichswehr 1930-1933," *Vierteljahrshefte für Zeitgeschichte*, vol. 2 (1954), pp. 434-35; Hossbach, *Zwischen Wehrmacht und Hitler*, pp. 181-92.

It was not a question of class privilege or of some sort of sociological power struggle. What Beck insisted upon throughout his career was that the political leadership must not make demands upon the armed forces that they could not meet, and that the political leadership must not get them into a position in which their very existence and that of the nation was threatened. If such a situation arose, Beck believed, the military leader was obliged "to resist with all means" the excessive demands made by the political leadership.[25] This consideration clarified the issue of who was primarily entitled to the military leader's loyalty. If impossible demands were made of the war-making potential of the German nation, loyalty to the head of state and Supreme Commander could amount to treason against the country; loyalty belonged first of all to the nation.

Even in cooperating in the expansion of the army beyond the limitations of Versailles to the extent suggested by the Second International Disarmament Conference in 1933, Beck objected to any suggestion of war (which, in his view, could only be a general war against many or most of the Allies of World War I). When the Army Office (*Allgemeines Heeresamt*) suggested the organization of an army of 300,000 men by October 1, 1934, Beck objected that this would amount to a mobilization, not to the development of a peacetime army. All he wanted for Germany was security. As Field Marshal Keitel put it during an interrogation in Nürnberg on August 27, 1945: "General Fritsch, Beck, only thought in terms of getting the German Army back on its feet. They only wanted to get the German Army back on its feet."[26] In characterizing the policies of Hitler's government, Beck wrote in April 1935: "It is not what we do, but how we do it that is so bad: policy of violence and perfidy."[27]

On May 2, 1935, as Chief of the Troop Office, Beck received a directive to prepare a "sudden attack," under code-name *Schulung*, against Czechoslovakia. His reaction was swift: he sent the directive on to General von Fritsch with a request to be relieved of his duties, "if it was contemplated to enter into practical preparations for war."[28] It was the position that Beck took again three years later, on the same issue, when it led to his final resignation. The reasons Beck offered against the preparation of *Schulung* did include some administrative argu-

[25] Ludwig Beck, *Studien*, ed. by Hans Speidel (Stuttgart: K. F. Koehler Verlag, [1955]), pp. 33-34, 60-61, 122; Foerster, *Generaloberst Ludwig Beck*, p. 32.

[26] Wilhelm Keitel, Testimony, Nürnberg, August 27, 1945, National Archives (Washington), Record Group No. 238.

[27] Bundesarchiv-Militärarchiv (Freiburg, i. Br.), N 28/2; Reynolds, *Treason Was No Crime*, p. 99; for correct wording, see German version: Nicholas Reynolds, *Beck: Gehorsam und Widerstand. Das Leben des deutschen Generalstabschefs 1935-1938* (Wiesbaden and Munich: Limes Verlag, 1977), p. 86.

[28] Müller, *Das Heer und Hitler*, p. 211; Reynolds, *Beck*, pp. 86-87 (incorrect in English ed.).

ments, but the principal objection was that Germany would become involved in a general war. In the absence of any information about the overall goals of a war such as the one envisaged by *Schulung*, it was not possible, Beck wrote on May 3, 1935, to produce correct strategic and tactical estimates; furthermore, it could not be assumed that an attack upon Czechoslovakia would remain isolated. It must be assumed that it would bring about an attack against German territory by the French army.

It has been maintained recently that Beck did not object to an attack on Czechoslovakia in principle, but only on the grounds that the German army would not be ready for it before about 1939-1940.[29] This is not supported by what Beck actually wrote. On the contrary, Beck made it clear that the contemplated attack was impossible not only at the present time but in future as well, and he continued to condemn the government's policy in general terms. In commenting on the May 2 directive he wrote on May 3 to Fritsch: "The thought of an operation such as *Schulung* can be considered as an aid in the conduct of war only for a later time if, apart from the required military groundwork, an improvement of the military-political situation, it is to be hoped, will have been achieved . . . ."[30] Notwithstanding the language Beck used here, he declared a war against Czechoslovakia an impossibility; he believed that any war between Germany and France which would necessarily result from a German attack on Czechoslovakia would, sooner or later, involve England and the United States.[31] When Göring had talked with the Hungarian head of state, Admiral Horthy, and the Hungarian Minister-President, Gömbös, about cooperation against Czechoslovakia, State Secretary von Bülow told Beck on June 22, 1935: "Any reasonably tolerable solution of the difficult Czech problem can be obtained only if the attackers have co-ordinated their plans in advance, and if the disinterest of third powers, or their immobilization, can be arranged beforehand."[32]

One obviously cannot expect military men to go on record as objecting to *any* kind of war on moral grounds. This would be asking them to deny their own reason for existence. But Beck and Fritsch came as close as could be expected. Both regarded as a national disaster any modern war that involved Germany.[33] Beck's conditions for an

[29] Reynolds, *Beck*, p. 88.

[30] Ibid., p. 87; cf. Herbert S. Levine, "The Mediator: Carl J. Burckhardt's Efforts to Avert a Second World War," *Journal of Modern History*, vol. 45 (1973), p. 442.

[31] Helmuth Groscurth, *Tagebücher eines Abwehroffiziers 1938-1940*, ed. by Helmut Krausnick and Harold C. Deutsch with Hildegard von Kotze (Stuttgart: Deutsche Verlags-Anstalt, 1970), pp. 474-83.

[32] Reynolds, *Beck*, p. 88.

[33] Max von Viebahn, "Generaloberst Ludwig Beck 29.6.1880-20.7.1944," signed typescript, June 29, 1948, p. 6.

attack on Czechoslovakia were such that they were not likely to be fulfilled. France would never enter into an alliance with Germany aiming at the destruction of Czechoslovakia, as far as anyone could see, nor would she consent to a German attack, nor could the Soviet Union be expected to accept a German invasion of Czechoslovakia. The factor of France alone was nearly certain to bring in Britain and eventually the United States, as Beck correctly predicted.[34] In any case, Beck flatly refused in 1935 to draft any plan for an attack on Czechoslovakia.

Early in 1937, particularly in May, the "Austrian problem" became a topic of acute interest. On May 20, 1937 Beck completed a memorandum for Fritsch in which he rejected any involvement of Germany in a European war, particularly one over Austria.[35] A war between only two of the European powers, Beck stated, was unthinkable. France at least, probably Poland as well, would be among the powers Germany might fight immediately if she attacked Czechoslovakia. Indeed, a French attack on Germany for some reason or pretext could not be ruled out, and Beck had been working, since 1935, on a contingency plan code-named *Rot*, which was designed to counter a French attack across the Rhine and to strengthen defences against Poland and Czechoslovakia.[36] On February 3, 1933, only a few days after his appointment as Chancellor, Hitler had told the leading military men of the *Reichswehr* that if France had statesmen, she would attack us *before* we rearm.[37] But when Beck received a directive issued by Blomberg on June 24, 1937 which included an order to prepare for a *Sonderfall Otto*, that is, for a German military intervention in Austria in case of a Habsburg restoration there, Beck refused to work out such a plan.[38] Lieutenant-General Wilhelm Keitel, then Chief of the *Wehrmacht* Office in the War Ministry, was soon sent to discuss the June 24 directive for *Rot* and for *Sonderfall Otto*. Beck told him: "The General Staff will make no such preparations [for *Sonderfall Otto*]."[39]

On March 9, 1938—after German pressures for a Nazi or pro-Nazi government there had become intense—the Austrian Chancellor Kurt

---

[34] See footnote 31 above.

[35] Foerster, *Generaloberst Ludwig Beck*, pp. 62-63; Müller, *Das Heer und Hitler*, p. 235.

[36] Foerster, *Generaloberst Ludwig Beck*, p. 61.

[37] Vogelsang.

[38] *Trial of the Major War Criminals before the International Military Tribunal: Nuremberg 14 November 1945-1 October 1946*, vol. 34 (Nuremberg: Secretariat of the Tribunal, 1949), pp. 732 et seq.; Müller, *Das Heer und Hitler*, p. 236.

[39] [Wilhelm Keitel], *Generalfeldmarschall Keitel: Verbrecher oder Offizier? Erinnerungen, Briefe, Dokumente des Chefs OKW*, ed. by Walter Görlitz (Göttingen, Berlin, and Frankfurt/M.: Musterschmidt-Verlag, [1961]), pp. 82, 95; Foerster, *Generaloberst Ludwig Beck*, pp. 61-63; Erich v[on] Manstein, *Aus einem Soldatenleben 1887-1939* (Bonn: Athenäum-Verlag, 1958), p. 325.

von Schuschnigg called for a referendum on March 13 in which Austrians were asked to declare themselves in favour of an independent Austria. On the same day, Hitler decided to invade Austria.[40] Probably among the motivating factors for the move at this point was the potentially explosive trial of Fritsch who in January had been (falsely) accused of homosexual misconduct. The first full session of the trial was to begin at 10:30 A.M. on March 10, 1938. At 10:00 A.M. Keitel, now Chief of *O.K.W.*, was summoned to the *Reich* Chancellery and ordered by Hitler to tell Beck to report at once on mobilization plans against Austria. Keitel evidently did not think he would be an effective messenger and suggested that he fetch Beck so that Hitler himself might give him his instructions. Beck came along, with his *Oberquartiermeister I*, Manstein, declaring that no preparations existed, and that he, Beck, could not accept any responsibility for a move against Austria. Hitler said Beck would not have to; he would have the *Schutzstaffel* (SS) invade Austria—if that was what the army wanted. In the face of a direct order, in the face of Hitler's threat to use the SS, and the menace of a Nazi takeover of the army, and with the Fritsch trial just begun, Beck had hardly any choice but to obey. Anything else would have amounted to mutiny or desertion. In any event, Czechoslovakia would be a better case on which to make a stand.

K.-J. Müller's contention that Beck gladly carried out Hitler's order because, finally, his long-standing demand for consultation by the head of state had been met, is untenable.[41] Beck himself made this clear in a letter to Hitler's former *Wehrmacht Adjutant*, Colonel Hossbach, in October 1938, when he referred to the interview of March 10 as those "accidental five minutes" apart from which Beck had never had an opportunity in his five years as Chief of the General Staff to speak to Hitler about his views on "territorial defence [*sic*], warfare, etc." Moreover, Beck, the new Commander-in-Chief of the Army, Brauchitsch, and Lieutenant-General von Viebahn, the Chief of *Wehrmacht* Leadership Staff (*Wehrmachtführungsstab*), far from carrying out orders gladly, all agonized through the night of March 11-12 over the dangers of an invasion of Austria. They bombarded Keitel with telephone calls demanding that he persuade Hitler to rescind his

---

[40] Max Domarus, *Hitler: Reden und Proklamationen 1932-1945*, 2 vols. paginated consecutively (Neustadt on Aisch: Verlagsdruckerei Schmidt, 1962-1963), p. 807; Keitel, *Testimony*; Keitel, *Generalfeldmarschall Keitel*, p. 178; Manstein, *Aus einem Soldatenleben*, p. 322, with incorrect date of March 7; Manstein's evidence in *Der Prozess gegen die Hauptkriegsverbrecher vor dem Internationalen Militärgerichtshof Nürnberg 14. November 1945-1. Oktober 1946*, vol. 20 (Nuremberg: Secretariat of the Tribunal, 1948), p. 658, with correct timing; see also Harold C. Deutsch, *Hitler and His Generals: The Hidden Crisis, January-June 1938* (Minneapolis: University of Minnesota Press, [1974]).

[41] Müller, *Das Heer und Hitler*, pp. 236-38; Hossbach, *Zwischen Wehrmacht und Hitler*, p. 193.

order.[42] Keitel promised to try but did not even tell Hitler of these representations.

The invasion of Czechoslovakia, *Fall Grün*, entered the stage of acute preparation immediately after the triumphant occupation of Austria; but, despite Beck's obstruction, it had been pursued in 1937 in the *Wehrmachtamt*, not in the General Staff of the army. On November 5, 1937, Hitler announced his intentions regarding Austria and Czechoslovakia to the Commanders-in-Chief of the armed forces without their Chiefs of Staff, to Foreign Minister von Neurath, and to Göring (Göring was Minister-President of Prussia, *Reich* Minister of Aviation, Commander-in-Chief of the *Luftwaffe*, and in charge of the Four Year Plan to prepare Germany for war).[43] On November 11, Hossbach, who had also been present, showed Beck his notes of what was said, and on November 12 Beck put his horrified reaction on paper, stating that while there might be a problem of space for Germany (with a view to the losses suffered in the Versailles Treaty, and with a view to a large German population living outside of German boundaries in Czechoslovakia), and while it might be necessary to solve the Czech problem (with a view to use of Czech airfields by military forces of the Soviet Union with preparations directed against Germany), this must not be done through war but through negotiation. A war would raise France and England against Germany, and Germany could not win a war against them. Beck did not deny, he said, the desirability of solving the Czech problem in favourable circumstances, and to engage in preparatory considerations—but before they could be entered into, he said, these would require a far more fundamental assessment of the overall situation than was evident from what was said at the conference of November 5, 1937.[44] Again, Beck rejected Hitler's plans. The Blomberg-Fritsch crisis and the *Anschluss* temporarily overshadowed the Czech problem, but Beck did not deviate from his position; nor did Hitler.

Meanwhile, since the conference of November 5, 1937, Keitel and Jodl (in charge of Territorial Defence Section, *Abteilung Landesverteidigung*, in *Allgemeines Wehrmachtamt*) were working on *Grün* and produced a new formulation of the directive by December 21, 1937.[45]

---

[42] Keitel, *Generalfeldmarschall Keitel*, p. 179; [Ernst Freiherr von Weizsäcker], *Die Weizsäcker-Papiere 1933-1950*, ed. by Leonidas Hill (Frankfurt/M., Berlin, and Vienna: Propyläen Verlag, 1974), p. 124.

[43] Hossbach, *Zwischen Wehrmacht und Hitler*, pp. 181-92; cf. Walter Bussmann, "Zur Entstehung und Überlieferung der 'Hossbach-Niederschrift,' " *Vierteljahrshefte für Zeitgeschichte*, vol. 16 (1968), pp. 373-84.

[44] Foerster, *Generaloberst Ludwig Beck*, pp. 80-82; Reynolds, *Treason Was No Crime*, p. 104, omits a good deal of Beck's substantive statements.

[45] *Trial of the Major War Criminals*, vol. 34 (1949), p. 754; *Akten zur deutschen auswärtigen Politik 1918-1945, Serie D (1937-1945)*, vol. 7 (Baden-Baden: Imprimerie Nationale,

It contained the sentence: "When Germany will have achieved her full war-readiness in all fields, the military precondition will have been created to conduct an aggressive war against Czechoslovakia and thereby to bring the solution of the German problem of space to a victorious end even if the one or other Great Power intervenes against us." On April 22, May 28 and 30, 1938, in oral addresses and in written directives, Hitler announced to commanding officers and staff officers of the army, navy, and air force his "unalterable decision to destroy Czechoslovakia by military action within a foreseeable time."[46] Beck reacted by submitting memoranda to Brauchitsch, the highest-ranking official in the state to whom he had access.

But now, having begun finally to understand fully the character of the National-Socialist regime, in the wake of the Blomberg-Fritsch crisis and in the face of the increasingly tense international situation, Beck went farther in his warnings of foreign intervention, and, before he stepped down, he went beyond anything he had expressed before in demanding that the army initiate a *coup d'état*.

In a memorandum of May 5, 1938, Beck concluded from an assessment of the strategic situation that the Czech problem could only be solved in a manner acceptable to Britain.[47] Brauchitsch, on Keitel's advice, reported only a part of the memorandum to Hitler, who rejected Beck's warnings out of hand. On May 29, the day after Hitler's oral announcement of his "unalterable decision," Beck wrote a further memorandum which reached Brauchitsch on May 30 and in which, after a scathing attack on Hitler's intentions and plans, Beck concluded that the Supreme Commander, Hitler, lacked competent advice and that there existed a leadership anarchy.[48] On the same May 30, Hitler issued his written orders to prepare the *Wehrmacht* for the attack on Czechoslovakia by October 1, and Beck submitted still another memorandum to Brauchitsch, on June 3, and again one on July 16, in which he warned that France and England would certainly intervene, and that their war aims would then not be limited to the restoration of Czech territory, but that they would wage "a life and death war against

---

1956), pp. 547-56. Misconceptions about what would solve the problem of space in Hitler's view were obviously widespread.

[46] *Trial of the Major War Criminals*, vol. 25 (1947), pp. 414-27; ibid., vol. 28 (1948), pp. 372-73; Müller, *Das Heer und Hitler*, pp. 300-44; *Trial of the Major War Criminals*, vol. 25 (1947), pp. 433-38, 445-47; Foerster, *Generaloberst Ludwig Beck*, p. 107.

[47] Foerster, *Generaloberst Ludwig Beck*, pp. 99-106; Müller, *Das Heer und Hitler*, pp. 300-307; Keitel, *Generalfeldmarschall Keitel*, p. 184 (incorrectly calling part 2 the military part).

[48] Foerster, *Generaloberst Ludwig Beck*, pp. 106-13; Helmut Krausnick, "Vorgeschichte und Beginn des militärischen Widerstandes gegen Hitler," *Vollmacht des Gewissens*, Europäische Publikation e.V., vol. 1 (Frankfurt/M. and Berlin: Alfred Metzner Verlag, 1960), pp. 310-12; Müller, *Das Heer und Hitler*, pp. 309-17.

Germany.''[49] Whatever Beck said in seemingly accepting the need to solve the Czech problem and the problem of German space was invalidated in the same breath, as it were, by the consequences he predicted in case of a German attack.

The essence of Hitler's policy was not the limited goal of the inclusion of three million Germans in the *Reich*, to be achieved through peaceful negotiations without military threat; in essence Hitler's policy was unlimited and reckless in both aims and methods. While any German nationalist and patriot could agree with the peaceful consolidation of the German-speaking populations left scattered by World War I, this was not at all what Hitler was driving at. Beck therefore told Brauchitsch on July 16 that the senior commanders of the *Wehrmacht* should threaten to resign in a body if Hitler persisted in his course: "History will indict these commanders with blood guilt if, in the light of their professional and political knowledge, they do not obey the dictates of their conscience. The soldier's duty to obey ends when his knowledge, his conscience and his responsibility forbid him to carry out a certain order."[50]

Beck knew that Hitler could not submit to such a protest without ceasing to be a dictator, and that only a *coup d'état* could produce the desired effect. On July 19 he demanded of Brauchitsch that immediately after the collective protest "there must be a thorough-going showdown between the *Wehrmacht* and the *SS*," and the "re-establishment of the rule of law," and on July 29, Beck again demanded a *coup d'état* and stated the consequences of the protest—a *coup d'état* in itself—most unequivocally.[51]

As Chief of the General Staff of the army, Beck had no command authority over troops. This authority belonged to the Commander-in-Chief and to those carrying out his orders. Brauchitsch, however, refused to lead or even to allow the protest that Beck demanded. Beck could hardly ask the senior commanders to refuse to obey the Commander-in-Chief and to follow him instead. It would have flown in the face of all that a military establishment must rely on, and it would have split the senior officer corps unevenly, most likely with the major-

---

[49] Foerster, *Generaloberst Ludwig Beck*, pp. 113-21; Müller, *Das Heer und Hitler*, pp. 312-13, 317-26; Gert Buchheit, *Ludwig Beck, ein preussischer General* (Munich: Paul List Verlag, 1964), pp. 147-55.

[50] Foerster, *Generaloberst Ludwig Beck*, pp. 121-23; Manstein, in *Trial of the Major War Criminals*, vol. 20 (1948), p. 624.

[51] Foerster, *Generaloberst Ludwig Beck*, pp. 124-27; Müller, *Das Heer und Hitler*, pp. 328-29; Krausnick, "Vorgeschichte und Beginn," p. 329; [Curt] Bernard, "Account," dated May 28, 1945, typescript, Institut für Zeitgeschichte (Munich), ED 106, vol. 90; Wilhelm Adam, "Eidesstattliche Erklärung Nr. 2: betrifft: Stimmung unter den höheren Generalstabsoffizieren bald nach der 'Machtergreifung,' " typescript, undated, Institut für Zeitgeschichte, ZS6; "Colonel-General Wilhelm Adam," typescript, undated (England, pre-1949); for the following two paragraphs, cf. Hoffmann, *History*, passim.

ity opting for Brauchitsch, not Beck. They would, in their majority, have followed a protest led by Brauchitsch and Beck, and in Brauchitsch's or Beck's absence, perhaps, by some other highly respected senior officer. But they could not be expected to act in a way that could divide the army against itself.

Since Brauchitsch refused to go along with the advice of his Chief of Staff on a most fundamental issue, Beck had no choice but to resign. He handed in his resignation on August 18, Hitler accepted it on August 21, and Beck turned over his office to his successor, General Halder, on August 27. As the most venerated military authority, Beck was involved in leading plots against Hitler throughout the war. On the evening of July 20, 1944, when the last plot had failed, he shot himself.

3

FIELD MARSHAL Erwin Rommel came to the same conclusions about Hitler as Beck, but considerably later and after quite a different sort of career. Rommel was born in Heidenheim in 1891. In World War I he served with great distinction in troop commands as a lieutenant. He welcomed the New Order in 1933. He was ambitious, and was honoured to be called upon to command the *Führer*'s Headquarters units. He questioned neither the *Führer*'s wisdom nor the policies which led to war when Hitler himself made him Major-General on the eve of World War II. At his own request, Rommel was given a division, the 7th Panzer, in 1940. He was put in command of the Africa Corps in February 1941; and in June 1942, at the age of fifty-one, he was made a Field Marshal. From January 1, 1944 he commanded Army Group B in France, with headquarters at La Roche-Guyon, was wounded on a visit to the front on July 17, 1944, and committed suicide at Hitler's strong suggestion on October 14, 1944.[52] His suicide was the result of his involvement in the secret opposition to Hitler. The remarks which follow will consider the nature and the depth of this involvement.

No precise moment can be pinpointed at which Rommel "joined" the opposition, in which "membership" was fluid and undefined. It is clear that he lost confidence in the outcome of the war and in Hitler's leadership, experiencing a fundamental reorientation, from about November 1942, leading to a conflict of loyalties. His assessment of Hitler became completely negative. He began to refer to him as a "criminal"; yet Hitler was the Supreme Commander of the *Wehrmacht* and the Commander-in-Chief of the army. The soldier's ethos and duty required obedience, but there was a duty, in Rommel's view, to his men as human beings with a just claim to life, with a right to be

---

[52] Peter Hoffmann, *Hitler's Personal Security* (Cambridge, Mass.: M.I.T. Press, 1979), p. 197; Irving, *Trail of the Fox*, passim; Keilig, *Das deutsche Heer*, 211/276.

protected against unreasonable demands, and there was a duty of
loyalty to the nation which now came into conflict with the duty to the
commander if the commander obviously led the armed forces and the
nation to their destruction. The conflict was compounded by the Allied
demand for "unconditional surrender" of the German armed forces,
and by what transpired of their postwar plans for Germany; this
appeared as only a different form of destruction. Rommel faced the
dilemma, but it was more than a year later before he got ready to act on
his conclusions.

At the beginning of November 1942, in North Africa, Rommel
told Major Elmar Warning, Ia officer in the staff of Colonel Westphal
of Panzer Group Africa: "Warning, believe me, Hitler is the greatest
criminal whom I know, he will fight not only to the last German soldier
but to the total destruction of Germany, in his own selfish interests."[53]
Later that month, Rommel flew, uninvited, to Hitler's headquarters in
East Prussia to tell him that Africa could not be held. He was received
most icily and told to mind his front.[54] It was then, as he said to a visitor
in August 1944, in hospital, that he had noticed that Hitler's intellectual
powers were failing.[55] During most of 1943 Rommel had no command
to speak of but was apparently very anxious to obtain one. Perhaps he
was more careful of what he said while his position was unclear; at any
rate there seem to be few statements regarding Hitler and the war that
have come down to posterity. In 1944, however, Rommel's verdicts on
Hitler's policy are no longer distinguishable from statements of opposition and of intention to act against the Supreme Commander and the
Commander-in-Chief; Rommel's statements now are more than mere
angry outbursts.

After Rommel had been given command of Army Group B in
France from January 1, 1944, he was considered a member of the
conspiracy according to his own intelligence officer, Colonel Staubwasser.[56] Rommel chose as his Chief of the General Staff Lieutenant-
General Hans Speidel, who arrived on April 15 at La Roche-Guyon
and told him that same evening what needed to be done to save
Germany: to end the war in the west, with or without Hitler's approval,
and eventually to "remove" Hitler himself since the Allies would never

---

[53] David Irving, Niederschrift eines Gesprächs mit Herrn Dir. Elmar Warning . . . ,
December 11, 1976, Selected Documents on the Life and Campaigns of Field-Marshal
Erwin Rommel, E.P. Microform Film, 97049/3; also see Irving, *Trail of the Fox*, p. 231,
where Rommel's verdict is suppressed.

[54] Irving, *Trail of the Fox*, pp. 245-48.

[55] David Irving, Notes on Second Interview with Herrn Oberbürgermeister Manfred Rommel . . . , June 7, 1975, Selected Documents of Field-Marshal Erwin Rommel.

[56] David Irving, Interview with Oberst i.G.a.D. Anton Staubwasser, May 31, 1975,
Selected Documents of Field-Marshal Erwin Rommel; Staubwasser, letter to David
Irving, Selected Documents of Field-Marshal Erwin Rommel, p. 12.

deal with him.[57] A steady stream of visitors now passed through La Roche-Guyon, some coming on their own initiative to visit the popular Field Marshal and to let him know that much of Germany looked to him with some vague hope that he take control of things, some brought there by Speidel, others arriving after Rommel had mentioned their names. Many came to impress upon Rommel the need for him to assume some "leading role" for the sake of "the future of Germany."[58] Rommel talked about what might be done and about the activities of the conspirators with Speidel, with his naval liaison officer, Admiral Ruge, with the Quartermaster General, General Eduard Wagner, with his artillery officer, Colonel Hans Lattmann, with Warning, with *Gauleiter* Karl Kaufmann of Hamburg, with Mayor Dr. Karl Strölin of Stuttgart, with Transport Minister Julius Dorpmüller. Strölin had talked high treason with Rommel in February 1944, and Rommel, looking for political support within the existing establishment for a change of regime, thinking that a few officers in Berlin were hardly enough to take over the *Reich* effectively and to maintain stability during a transition period with continuing hostilities, conferred with the Hamburg *Gauleiter*, Kaufmann, and with Dorpmüller in the weeks before the Allied invasion of Normandy (June 6). Rommel talked of "political consequences" after the invasion which was certain to bring about the defeat of Germany.[59] On May 15, Rommel conferred with the *Wehrmacht* Commander who headed the occupation administration in France, General von Stülpnagel, with both Chiefs of Staff present, about measures to be taken to end the war in the west unilaterally, and to overthrow the Nazi regime.[60] General Wagner came to coordinate measures for the *coup d'état* in the west with those prepared in the *Reich*, and for the first time he told Rommel of the attempts on Hitler's life already made by members of the conspiracy.[61] Rommel expressed himself as opposed to assassination because he did not want Hitler to become a martyr; he wanted him arrested and put on trial. In

[57] Friedrich Ruge (Vizeadmiral, Marineverbindungsoffizier bei HGr B, GFM Rommel, Ob., Ia M), Tagebuch geführt beim Stabe der Heeresgruppe B (Fm. Rommel) 20.12.1943-1.8.1944, Selected Documents of Field-Marshal Erwin Rommel, E.P. Microform Film 97049/2 (also in Institut für Zeitgeschichte), June 25, 1944 et seq., July 15, 1944; Hans Speidel, *Invasion 1944: Ein Beitrag zu Rommels und des Reiches Schicksal*, 3rd ed. (Tübingen: Rainer Wunderlich Verlag Hermann Leins, 1950), pp. 77-84; Eduard Wagner, *Der Generalquartiermeister: Briefe und Tagebuchaufzeichnungen* (Munich and Vienna: Günther Olzog Verlag, 1963), p. 233.

[58] Irving, Selected Documents of Field-Marshal Erwin Rommel, passim.

[59] Karl Kaufmann, information given to the author on January 15, 1965; Irving, *Trail of the Fox*, pp. 417-18, 426; Wagner, *Der Generalquartiermeister*, p. 233.

[60] Speidel, *Invasion 1944*, p. 84; Wagner, *Der Generalquartiermeister*, p. 233.

[61] Speidel, *Invasion 1944*, p. 84; Wagner, *Der Generalquartiermeister*, p. 233; Gen. d. Panzertruppen Heinrich Eberbach, letter to Militärgeschichtliches Forschungsamt (Freiburg i.Br.), April 11, 1967, Selected Documents of Field-Marshal Erwin Rommel.

discussions with Lieutenant-Colonel von Hofacker, a cousin of Stauffenberg, and Dr. Max Horst, a brother-in-law of Speidel, he took the same position regarding S.S. leaders who were to be arrested in Paris. Both Hofacker and Horst held positions in the military administration of occupied France, Hofacker as a liaison officer in Stülpnagel's staff charged with maintaining the connections and coordination between the Berlin conspiracy, Stülpnagel's staff, Rommel's staff, and the staff of Supreme Commander West Field Marshal von Rundstedt (Kluge from July 4).[62] Rommel was again informed fully by Hofacker, on July 9, of all the essential details of the plot, including the planned assassination of Hitler, to which he raised no objection at that point.[63] This was after a visit Hitler had paid to the western theatre of war on June 17, on which occasion Rommel had demanded "political consequences" to be drawn from the hopeless military situation and had been told brusquely to mind his front. It was also after a visit by Rommel to Hitler's "Berghof" retreat on Obersalzberg on June 29, where Hitler had ordered the Field Marshal literally "to leave the room" when Rommel had tried twice to talk about the "political situation," and finally "about Germany."[64]

Now Rommel was telling numerous people that he intended to make a deal with the Western Allies to conclude an armistice in the west and then to march against the Russians, even against Hitler's will.[65] When Warning wondered, about the middle of July, what could be done if Hitler refused to end the fighting in the west as Rommel was going to request of him once again, Rommel said: "Then I shall open the Western front, because there is only one important decision, namely to see to it that the Anglo-Americans will be in Berlin before the Russians!"[66] On July 15 Rommel signed a teletype message addressed to the *Führer*, an "ultimatum" as Rommel called it, adding in his own

---

[62] Walter Bargatzky, "Persönliche Erinnerungen an die Aufstandsbewegung des 20. Juli 1944 in Paris," roneoed typescript, Baden-Baden, October 20, 1945; Peter Hoffmann, *Widerstand, Staatsstreich, Attentat: Der Kampf der Oppostion gegen Hitler*, 3rd rev. and expanded ed. (Munich: R. Piper Verlag, 1979), pp. 432-36.

[63] Wilhelm Keitel, Testimony, September 28, 1945, Nuremberg, National Archives RG 238; Dr. Gotthard Freiherr von Falkenhausen, letter to Dr. Clemens Plassmann, March 24, 1947; Friedrich Freiherr von Teuchert, [Aufzeichnungen über den 20. Juli 1944], typescript, Munich, [1946], p. 13; Elmar Michel, "Pariser Erinnerungen," typescript, undated, Institut für Zeitgeschichte Archiv Nr. 860/53.

[64] Speidel, *Invasion 1944*, pp. 126-27; Irving, *Trail of the Fox*, pp. 398-99; David Irving, Notes on an Interview of Major a.D. Eberhard Wolfram, June 1, 1976, Selected Documents of Field-Marshal Erwin Rommel.

[65] David Irving, Interview with Oberst Hans Lattmann, June 15, 1975, Selected Documents of Field-Marshal Erwin Rommel; Ruge, July 2 and 13, 1944, Selected Documents of Field-Marshal Erwin Rommel.

[66] Warning, Selected Documents of Field-Marshal Erwin Rommel; Ruge, July 4 and 13, 1944, Selected Documents of Field-Marshal Erwin Rommel.

hand a sentence on "political consequences" of the military situation in the west. The teletype message was not sent before Rommel was wounded two days later, but Kluge had it sent on to *Führer* headquarters after July 20.[67] At the same time that Rommel decided on this ultimatum, the Field Marshal had begun asking field commanders what they would do if they received orders from him contradicting those of Hitler. On July 17, hours before Rommel was wounded, the commander of the 1st S.S. Panzer Corps, Sepp Dietrich, gave this answer: "You're the boss, Herr Feldmarschall, I obey only you—whatever it is you're planning."[68]

Rommel had told Hitler on several occasions what he thought, but even after the July 20 attack, Hitler was reluctant to brand the popular Field Marshal a traitor, and to cause other Field Marshals and Generals to think if even Rommel turned against the *Führer*, there was nothing to be done but desert the Nazi cause. Both Rommel and Hitler knew well that what Rommel had been doing was treason in the eyes of Hitler, and although the *Gestapo* seems to have dismissed as spurious the first indication it received that Rommel was involved in the plot, the evidence against him soon began to accumulate.[69] Colonel Hansen, Chief of the remnants of Canaris' *Abwehr* organization now incorporated in *Reichssicherheitshauptamt VI Mil* under Schellenberg, reported, under *Gestapo* interrogation, what he had learned from Hofacker about the latter's conversations with Rommel and Kluge in which, as Hofacker had reported on July 16, they had supported the conspiracy; Rommel's ultimatum became known about the same time. On August 1, Jodl wrote in his diary: "The *Führer* asks me to read a report from Kaltenbrunner on the testimony of Lieutenant-Colonel von Hofacker about his talks with K. and R. The *Führer* is now looking for a new Commander-in-Chief West. He plans to question R.[ommel] after his recovery, and then to retire him without any further fuss."[70] Hitler apparently found the Hofacker story more believable than the *Gestapo* had dared to. Then the civilian leader of the conspiracy, Dr. Goerdeler, who was arrested on August 12 also seems to have implicated the two Field Marshals.[71] On August 14 Himmler reported to Hitler concerning Goerdeler's arrest, and also concerning "West. Kluge-Rommel."[72]

---

[67] Speidel, *Invasion 1944*, pp. 137-41, 175-77; Irving, *Trail of the Fox*, p. 412.

[68] Wagner, *Der Generalquartiermeister*, p. 233; Irving, *Trail of the Fox*, pp. 417-18, 428.

[69] *Spiegelbild einer Verschwörung: Die Kaltenbrunner-Berichte an Bormann und Hitler über das Attentat vom 20. Juli 1944. Geheime Dokumente aus dem ehemaligen Reichssicherheitshauptamt* (Stuttgart: Seewald Verlag, 1961), p. 101; see also footnote 74 below.

[70] Irving, *Trail of the Fox*, p. 428.

[71] [Carl Friedrich Goerdeler], "Unsere Idee," typescript, November 1944, p. 30, Bundesarchiv Nl Goerdeler 26; Hoffmann, *History*, p. 516.

[72] Heinrich Himmler, Notes on conferences with Hitler and others, manuscript,

On August 15, all contact with Kluge was lost for hours when he had gone into the Falaise area and had lost his radio truck through enemy fire; Kluge was immediately suspected of desertion and treason and was replaced by Field Marshal Model without notice.[73] By August 31, Hitler spoke of Kluge's treason as an established fact—Kluge had been summoned to Berlin after he had returned from his front visit but had taken his own life on the way back to Germany.[74]

Rommel's position and involvement in the plot were by this time, in Keitel's words, "not ambiguous."[75] Only then his former Chief of the General Staff, Lieutenant-General Speidel, was relieved on September 5. He visited Rommel at his home near Ulm on September 6 and was arrested on September 7.[76] It is clear that he could not have told the *Gestapo* anything essential that they did not already know about Rommel's involvement. Nor did he tell them, as David Irving maintained recently despite the evidence to the contrary, that *he* knew anything about the conspiracy, or else he could not have been rescued from the *Gestapo* by the military Court of Honour which was set up to expel suspected plotters from the *Wehrmacht* so that they passed under civil "justice." Not only was it impossible to "betray" any of Rommel's thoughts which the latter had revealed to Hitler in person previously; there is also direct evidence from Keitel and Jodl that Speidel had not implicated Rommel. Keitel said under interrogation on September 28, 1945: "No, certainly not from Speidel."[77] Speidel only confirmed Hofacker's visit of July 9, which was also confirmed, still according to Keitel, by "all members of his [Rommel's] staff." It would not have been possible to conceal this visit without causing dozens of people to be silent about it. Irving's constant allusions to Speidel's testimony implicating Rommel all refer to the same thing: Speidel's confirmation of Hofacker's visit as such, but without any revelations about what was said.[78] Jodl stated on October 2, 1945: "I also read the testimony of Speidel, the Chief of Staff of Rommel. He stated that he had no knowledge of the substance of the conversation [of Hofacker with Rommel]."[79] Keitel was presiding during the Court of Honour proceed-

---

May 1934-December 1944, Bundesarchiv NS 19/275, NS 19/331, and National Archives, microfilm T-175, roll 94, fr. 2615328, August 14, 1944.

[73] Keitel, Testimony, September 28, 1945.

[74] Helmut Heiber (ed.), *Hitlers Lagebesprechungen: Die Protokollfragmente seiner militärischen Konferenzein 1942-1945* (Stuttgart: Deutsche Verlags-Anstalt, 1962), p. 620; Hoffmann, *History*, pp. 519, 529.

[75] Keitel, Testimony, September 28, 1945.

[76] Speidel, *Invasion 1944*, pp. 71, 176.

[77] Keitel, Testimony, September 28, 1945.

[78] Manfred Rommel, "Rommels Tod," *Südkurier* (Konstanz), September 8, 1945; Dr. Max Horst, in Irving, *Trail of the Fox*, p. 435.

[79] Alfred Jodl, Testimony, October 2, 1945, Nuremberg, National Archives, RG 238.

ings against Speidel, and in his interrogations after the war he did not recall any evidence against Speidel given during these proceedings.

During the Court of Honour proceedings, however, Keitel tried quite hard to have Speidel convicted—a fact he did not mention in his postwar interrogation.[80] A member of the Court, Lieutenant-General Heinrich Kirchheim, swore after the war that Kaltenbrunner, acting as prosecutor against the absent defendant, accused Speidel of having admitted that he had known of the assassination plan through an officer in Stülpnagel's staff, that he had informed Rommel of this, and that he had not done anything further because he claimed he did not know that Rommel had not reported his information. Still according to Kirchheim, Keitel then added that the *Führer* thought Speidel's guilt could not be doubted. In any regular court, according to Western standards, this would have been regarded as undue influence and prejudicial; it weighed much more heavily in Hitler's police state. Kirchheim and Colonel-General Guderian, who was also a member of the Court on October 4, 1944 when Speidel's case was heard, both reported that they stated they did not consider Speidel guilty, and that Keitel and Kaltenbrunner then said that, if Speidel was not guilty, as they, Kirchheim and Guderian, maintained, there was at least suspicion against him.[81] This amounted to an admission that Kaltenbrunner's accusations were either not true at all, or the interpretation given to them by Kaltenbrunner and Keitel was wholly arbitrary.

4

W HEN LIEUTENANT-COLONEL von Hofacker spoke with Field Marshal Rommel on July 9, 1944 and informed him of the details of the conspiracy, he mentioned the name Tauroggen: a place that every German officer who had ever attended the War Academy was familiar with as representing disobedience in the interest of loyalty of a higher

---

[80] For this and the following: Heinrich Kirchheim, "Eidesstattliche Erklärung," typescript, Neustadt/Kr. Marburg, September 16, 1947, Institut für Zeitgeschichte, ED 100; Keitel, Testimony, September 28, 1945.

[81] Heinz Guderian, "Eidesstattliche Erklung," typescript, Neustadt/Kr. Marburg, September 10, 1947, Institut für Zeitgeschichte, ED 100; Kirchheim, letter to H. Guderian (son), October 23, 1965, Institut für Zeitgeschichte, ED 100. Irving ignores Keitel's and Jodl's testimony in this context, and he does not fully use that of Kirchheim and Guderian. While failing to accept uncontradicted testimony, he attempts to make a case against Speidel by innuendo and by citing Speidel's brother-in-law, Dr. Max Horst, for the contents of a sheet of paper on which Horst was shown only the signature of Hofacker and Speidel, with the text itself covered up! See Irving, *Trail of the Fox*, pp. 396-444, esp. pp. 429, 434-35. At least one former member of Rommel's staff, Colonel Staubwasser, accused Irving of disregarding and misrepresenting evidence; Staubwasser, letter to Irving, May 1976, Selected Documents of Field-Marshal Erwin Rommel, E. P. Microform Film 97049/3.

order than formal adherence to specific directives.[82] Perhaps it was an accident that Hofacker was a cousin of Claus Graf Stauffenberg, whose mother was a great-granddaughter of General Graf von Gneisenau, Chief of the General Staff to Marshal Blücher in 1814-1815, during the victorious phase of the Wars of Liberation against Napoleon's rule that were initiated for Prussia by what occurred at Tauroggen. Perhaps it was an accident that a descendant of the Prussian General Yorck who had signed the Convention of Tauroggen with the Russians on December 30, 1812 neutralizing the Prussian troops under Yorck's command, cooperated closely with Stauffenberg in the conspiracy against Hitler and was among the leading conspirators in Graf Moltke's Kreisau Group for years. Perhaps the presence of all these and many other historical names—Peter Graf Yorck von Wartenburg, Helmuth James Graf von Moltke, Claus Graf Schenk von Stauffenberg, Fritz-Dietlof Graf von der Schulenburg, Axel Freiherr von dem Bussche, Erwin von Witzleben—was more than a mere accident. It was certainly no accident that disobedience in the face of orders given irresponsibly, disobedience under the dictate of the human conscience, continued to be practised by members of the highest military ranks. In fact, in the interest of saving Germany and her people from foreign occupation and from further ravages of war, Rommel's thoughts had been following a "Tauroggen" pattern when he hoped to reach an agreement with the Western Allies for a truce in the west and for keeping the Russians out of Germany. Beck's hopes had had the same tendency for some time longer than Rommel's, but Beck had gone beyond such hopes: he had accepted not only the inevitability of Germany's defeat but also that of "unconditional surrender" to all the Allies, and of the military occupation of Germany by Allied troops.[83] Both Rommel and Beck were, each in his own way, rooted in German military tradition. In this tradition, disobedience under the dictate of the conscience was not a new phenomenon but based on ancient concepts of the right to resist misused authority. This tradition of disobedience was based on the most fundamental ethos of the soldier and the man. In the last resort, insofar as the plotters barely expected to succeed, this ethos led them to self-sacrifice, if not for the sake of the physical integrity of their country then certainly for the sake of the restoration of the moral integrity and honour of their nation.[84]

---

[82] Peter Paret, *Yorck and the Era of Prussian Reform 1807-1815* (Princeton, N.J.: Princeton University Press, 1966), pp. 191-96; *Gothaisches Genealogisches Taschenbuch der Gräflichen Häuser Teil A 109. Jahrgang 1936* (Gotha: Justus Perthes, [1935]), p. 591; *Genealogisches Handbuch des Adels*, vol. 10: *Genealogisches Handbuch der gräflichen Häuser, Gräfliche Häuser A*, vols. 2 and 3 (Glücksburg/Ostsee: Verlag von C. A. Starke, 1955, 1958), vol. 2, pp. 391-95, vol. 3, p. 444; Hoffmann, *Widerstand, Staatsstreich, Attentat*, pp. 446-58.

[83] Hoffmann, *History*, pp. 375-76.

[84] Peter Hoffmann, *Widerstand gegen Hitler: Probleme des Umsturzes* (Munich: R. Piper Verlag, 1979), passim.

General Albert C. Wedemeyer is an eminently qualified observer of the military opposition to Hitler. He had attended the German War Academy in the 1930s and knew the bearers of the famous names personally. He wrote in 1951:

> Colonel-General Ludwig Beck... and scores of other senior and junior officers deplored Nazi racial discrimination, the unscrupulous acts of aggression, and the rule of tyranny as epitomized by Hitler and his henchmen. I knew General Beck personally and considered him one of the finest men I have met in any country—a cultured gentleman, enlightened and tolerant. General Beck, General Rommel, and thousands of other patriotic Germans in the military service were understandably in a most difficult position, torn between sworn loyalties to those in power and their innate loyalties to principles of decency and justice in human relationships.[85]

---

[85] A. C. Wedemeyer, Review of Speidel, *Invasion 1944*, in *The Annals of The American Academy of Political and Social Science*, vol. 274 (1951), pp. 218-19.

INDEX

DATE DUE

DEC 1 3			
OCT 0 5 1999			